MIND MAPPING

How to Create Mind Maps Step-by-step

(The Best Way to Improve Memory, Creativity, Concentration & More)

Martin Thompson

Published By Bella Frost

Martin Thompson

All Rights Reserved

Mind Mapping: How to Create Mind Maps Step-by-step (The Best Way to Improve Memory, Creativity, Concentration & More)

ISBN 978-1-77485-302-3

All rights reserved. No part of this guide may be reproduced in any form without permission in writing from the publisher except in the case of brief quotations embodied in critical articles or reviews.

Legal & Disclaimer

The information contained in this book is not designed to replace or take the place of any form of medicine or professional medical advice. The information in this book has been provided for educational and entertainment purposes only.

The information contained in this book has been compiled from sources deemed reliable, and it is accurate to the best of the Author's knowledge; however, the Author cannot guarantee its accuracy and validity and cannot be held liable for any errors or omissions. Changes are periodically made to this book. You must consult your doctor or get professional medical advice before using any of the suggested remedies, techniques, or information in this book.

Upon using the information contained in this book, you agree to hold harmless the Author from and against any damages, costs, and expenses, including any legal fees potentially resulting from the application of any of the information provided by this guide. This disclaimer applies to any damages or injury caused by the use and application, whether directly or indirectly, of any advice or information presented, whether for breach of contract, tort, negligence, personal injury, criminal intent, or under any other cause of action.

You agree to accept all risks of using the information presented inside this book. You need to consult a professional medical practitioner in order to ensure you are both able and healthy enough to participate in this program.

TABLE OF CONTENTS

INTRODUCTION 1

CHAPTER 1: ESSENTIALS OF MIND MAPS 4

CHAPTER 2: USING INDICATORS 10

CHAPTER 3: DECIDE AND ATTAIN YOUR GOALS 20

CHAPTER 4: MIND MAPPING SOFTWARE 38

CHAPTER 5: MIND MAPPING TOOLS 52

CHAPTER 6: THE BENEFITS OF MIND MAPPING 69

CHAPTER 7: MIND MAPPING EXAMPLES 82

CHAPTER 8: BENEFITS OF USING MIND MAPS 89

CHAPTER 9: GOAL SETTING AND MAKING PLANS WITH MIND MAPS 106

CHAPTER 10: TIPS TO UTILIZE A MIND MAP 122

CHAPTER 11: ASK FOR ASSISTANCE WITH YOUR IDEAS . 142

CHAPTER 12: WHAT TO CUSTOMIZE A MIND MAP 146

CHAPTER 13: DIGITAL MIND MAPS 156

CHAPTER 14: THE BENEFITS OF MAKING USE OF MIND MAPS 169

CHAPTER 15: EXAMPLES OF MIND MAPPING AND MIND MAPPING SOFTWARE 179

Introduction

You may be a student and need to note notes quickly and efficiently during classes or a business professional who needs to understand the ways that different aspects of their business work together or just a person who is capable of thinking more clear about their lives Mind mapping is an excellent tool for doing it!

The mind map is way of making notes and connecting ideas that helps you connect and visualize concepts more efficiently than any other note-taking method ever invented. The reason why mind maps work is because they reflect (copy) our way of thinking. think naturally. Normal notes are linear; they are arranged in a list , and ideas that are similar could be a few Bullet points (or webpages!) apart. It isn't something that is natural and simple to understand for the brain. Computers are able to easily connect ideas that are far away physically, but the human brain functions more effectively when thinking in hierarchies that are logical groups and subgroupings of concepts.

Mind maps are visual representation system that begins with a central concept that is drawn on the middle of the page. Then it expands out by focusing on the major ideas that connect to the main theme. The branches then are their own branches. the branches of those branches also have branches, and the list goes further...

The mind map can also provide different ways to keep things organized and easy to recall. Each of the branches on the map contain just one name (usually) for each. This makes it possible to have greater branches and connections that make the information more effective. It has been said we don't have the ability to learn something isn't something we already know. It doesn't mean we're doomed to be inactive, however what it means is that you learn through associations and when we are having difficulties connecting something with the knowledge we have, it is difficult recalling the information and applying it in our daily lives. Mind mapping aids in this connection and is the reason it's so efficient.

Within the system of mind maps I will be teaching you, I am also going to incorporate a method to label each branch of the mind map using symbols that makes it easier to look at the map's mind and quickly determine what a branch is something to do with facts, statistics, figures, fascinating ideas, people, etc...

Chapter 1: Essentials Of Mind Maps

A mind map is an image that results after a lengthy brainstorming session on a specific issue or issue. It is the process of writing down your thoughts in the form of graphic images or representations to create an accurate picture of the subject or issue of concern.

The principles that are involved in the mind map and its mindmaps have been used for a long time. These concepts encompass notes, learning visual thinking, problem solving , and brainstorming. They are used by educators, engineers psychologists, educators, and many other professions that require extensive thinking prior to coming to an agreement. Mind maps have been utilized to create thinking for years now. It was first evident in around the third century BC. Porphyry of Tyros who was a philosopher is thought as the one who was first person to utilize mind mapping to generate concepts that helped others learn faster.

Another person who is a fan of brain mapping and brainstorming can be found in Ramaon Llull. The man is Catalan philosopher and the creator of the first well-known writing in Catalan literature. Leonardo da Vinci is also thought to have utilized mind mapping in his note-taking sessions. The historians say that Da Vinci is often considered as the person who made mind mapping a popular concept.

Mind mapping evidence was discovered by historians years following Da Vinci at the latter half of 1950s. This was the time when the notion of network semantics is thought to have developed. Network semantics is thought of as a theory that helps learners in their development. It was later endorsed by Ross Quillian as well as Dr. Alan Collins who was later regarded as the originator of modern-day mapping. The reason for this was his increasing determination to publish research papers on learning and graphic thinking. Quillian as well as Collins were said to be the architects of the future of mind mapping as they created a kind of network in which every concept and idea was connected through links. Links show the way in which a particular object is connected to an additional. In the present mind mapping has become extremely popular in sharing ideas, learning as well as other forms of collaboration. But, the popularity of using mind maps was at its highest in the late 1960s and Tony Buzan, a British psychologist. Buzan developed a set of guidelines, to be followed during the use of the mind map.

Beyond professional fields Mind mapping is also utilized in high schools and colleges and universities. Many mind maps are made using software for mind mapping, which makes the process much easier. There are few people who prefer to draw them with paper. Mind mapping software reduces the time required to draw things following rearrangements and modifications. It just provides the hyperlinks based on inputs and then places them in specific regions of the mind map. Additionally, the mind mapping software can be found as cloud-based or web-based tools or as an independent application . Other mind mapping applications are accessible via smartphones, which makes it simple for people to create their own mind maps at any time and from wherever they'd like.

The significance

A lot of people doubt the reason of mind maps and whether they are useful or beneficial. Of course, they can be beneficial when brainstorming is needed. For instance, you may have had a great idea before writing an essay. But, when you attempted to record your thoughts and you were feeling like your idea had run out. Maybe you've also thought that your thoughts don't make sense in any way.

This is often the case when you haven't organized your work correctly and have created every possible idea related to this type of work. That's why mind maps are important and beneficial.

A mind map is generally thought to be a fundamental idea that is able to be divided into several themes or ideas. The process is executed by using colored pencils or markers. These tools are often used to provide guidelines in determining where ideas are derived from. In addition, they assist in the re-evaluation of all ideas. Mind mapping can be described as a method for note-taking that includes diagrams that serve in visual tools. Mind maps are easy to create and mastering mind mapping is easy. It can help simplify your job significantly. When you write down your thoughts in this way, you are using the left part of your brain it is more of an analytical. The left part of the brain is limited to thinking creatively and is only able to hold only one idea at a. However the right side your brain is ideal for mapping your mind. It is the visual portion that the brain uses. So, using a mind map will allow you to get the entire image of your thoughts immediately. It will also help you be able to avoid the process of analysis that typically allow you to focus on just one idea at a.

It is not necessary to be an expert and creative author. Utilizing a mind map properly will allow you to generate amazing ideas. Mind maps are an essential tool for brainstorming and the process of collaborating images and words, producing amazing results.

Chapter 2: Using Indicators

The techniques described in this chapter were influenced by a different note-taking system called"the bullet journal. Bullet journals are an analog note-taking. It allows you to organize the present, past and future.

Making use of the bullet journaling in your mind maps can be beneficial to incorporate more details to your small space

Bullet journals are an instrument to note down your thoughts and record the things that you need to remember however there's an intriguing idea that we can integrate into our mental diagrams to help them be more effective

The idea we will incorporate is known as "Signifiers" They are tiny symbols like an asterisk , an exclamation point, smiley face or a smiley face. We will use them in every notepad to ensure that when we're searching for a particular kind of concept, all we have to do is look for the signs. As an example, you may be able to identify good ideas, quotes, be used in a test as well as inspirational thoughts or discussion points... And as you become more familiar with them, you'll be able identify more opportunities to utilize these.

If you're using a journal to record all your mind maps, it's an excellent idea to keep your markers on the back, like a key to the map. You can then revisit them regularly and ensure that you're making use of them regularly. This idea is among my top ways to enhance the power of mind maps as it allows you to find the information quickly.

Here is a checklist of indicators:

- idea you like

An idea that can make you feel sad

*point to be remembered

! Brilliant point!

!! Excellent point!

? Discussion topic

?? Something that you don't agree with

The % statistic is important to keep in mind

"..." Quotes are written at the bottom of the page

Thought bubbles - ideas that are original to be added

Feel free to add more information to the list of signs and put them to the opposite side of the words you recorded. Utilizing signifiers frequently will dramatically enhance the quality of your notes will be during a review because you'll have access to every idea you'd like to think of.

If you must and should not be using mind maps

Mind maps are fantastic tools nine percent of the time, they offer a superior alternative to traditional note-taking however, as with any tool, there's a right time and place to utilize it, as well as an appropriate time and place not to. Mind maps are fantastic to connect diverse ideas and keeping an eye on ideas that do not flow in a sequential manner. Mind maps are also great to organize ideas that don't have to be reconstructed in full sentences and concepts that aren't able to be absorbed in a hurry.

The biggest drawback of minds maps lies in the fact that they're not effective to capture full sentences. The fact that they're a bit slower . The most important times to return to normal note-taking
If you're in a fast-paced class
If you're a instructor in your the college classroom or as part of an ongoing education program in the field of business, then mind mapping can turn into an absolute nightmare. Certain people be awed by the speed of their presentations and ad nauseum with more information than you can possibly how to handle. If they speak this quickly, the problem can be that they don't leave the time to consider how to manage all the data... due to the fact that you're too busy trying to record the entire thing! !

I can remember a theatre teacher I had, and she was notorious for her habit of presenting her classes as a bullet-point list of essential ideas that she would be reading as quick as feasible (or at least it seemed like) all of the students was looking at their notebooks in a frantic fashion taking notes and trying that they could keep pace. It was not unusual that me and the students closest to me would utilize 3-4 pages to write notes over an time of an hour.

The most effective solution for situations like this is to make notes as you normally would and later at home, you can transform the notes into an organized mind map. It is typical for this to take about 30 minutes but you'll end up with the main points of the presentation you attended at , and the map will be much superior to the muddled note-taking jumble you had to jumble to put together at the time.

The majority of the lecture is in the form of long phrases or quotations

If you're taking a class on something you're not well-versed in, you'll be amazed by the sheer number of terms, names for places or events names, item names and so on... that are required to record with an explanation. It's not a problem with this, however when a lecture is filled with more than a few of these terms, a mind map doesn't make sense. We have discussed earlier the possibility of citing quotations on a separate piece of paper. However, if the lecture contains greater than about 25% of the time, normal linear notes are more appropriate.

4 Uses for mind maps

Life Planning

One of the most effective ways to use mind mapping is to map out the various aspects of your life, and what you want them to appear. I've had huge success in enhancing my ideas about my future by using mind mapping. Thanks to the generative and imaginative way in which mind mapping can be used, I came up with a variety of ways to enhance my life than I have ever thought of just simply by sitting and performing this easy life activity. If you've never sat down to reflect on your life , I strongly suggest you try the next exercise to gain a feel about the potential of the mind map to contemplate your goals.

Step one: open your favorite program or notebook open

Step 2: Draw yourself on the middle of your mind map.

3. On the initial stage, list every aspect of your life you could make better and really work to create as numerous ideas as you're capable of: mental and physical health and finances, friendships, love , travel, etc...

Step 4: Brainstorm what success means to you in these areas, what's you ideal shape, what is your dream type of relationship and so on...

Step five: when you've got a picture of what you desire, begin to think of every possible thing you can do to get there.

Sixth step, looking back through the entire map, mark an asterisk at the top of every idea or ways to achieve your goal that you are planning to employ.

Step seven: reread your mind map frequently and even daily.

Book outline

One of the greatest ways to use Mind mapping can be to sketch out books to truly get to the core of the text as quickly as is possible. Being that the books are divided into chapters makes laying them out on your mind map simple.

Step one: Go through the book, going through every paragraph for each chapter. Then, decide which of chapters you want to go through. Most books will have 5 useful, informative chapters while the rest are mostly uninteresting or repeats the same information repeatedly.

Step 2 Step two: Draw the book on center of the map, with the branches for every one chapter that you'll read.

Step 3: Go through the chapters you've chosen by reading the first sentence or every paragraph until you get an idea that is really great when that happens, go through the idea , and put it in the right branch of your mental map.

Step four: Go over your mind map to ensure that all the main concepts are covered and there's nothing you don't comprehend.

This method of reading the book may appear somewhat unusual at first , and you might feel as if you're not getting the information of the book that you haven't.

However, covering a book from cover the cover is a standard that we all adhere to, but it isn't an absolute rule. by only reading the most important portions of the book, you're capable of retaining the most important information, and can understand the book more quickly and in a shorter amount of time than the average person.

Lectures

We've talked a lot about how to utilize mind maps to note notes during lectures, but a humorous and intriguing point must be discussed. Drawing a cartoon of your instructor in the center the mindmap can help! While this may sound funny it is, a well-drawn caricature does more than any other image I've seen (and perhaps it will help you as well!)

Finding solutions to issues

Utilizing mind maps to find solutions to the issues you're confronted with is among the best methods to conquer difficulties that appear to be insurmountable. Through a mindmap, you will be able to break down a problem into its constituent components and reconstruct it in a way that helps you find an answer quickly and effortlessly.

Step 1 Note down the issue you're dealing with on the mind map.

Step 2: Write down the reasons why this is a problem, as well as some of the negative impacts of it at the beginning stage on the chart.

Step Three: Write down possible solutions to the symptoms of the issue in the next branches of the mind map.

Step four: go through every way you can alleviate the symptoms and then ask yourself "Is there a way I could improve all these symptoms simultaneously?"

You'll be amazed at how often just gaining a amount of perspective in the subject and focusing on the various elements can help you create a feasible solution.

Chapter 3: Decide and Attain Your Goals

Anyone who has an "why," which serves as an objective, a finality and a way to deal with the "how." Nietzsche

These are the times when we're you are at work, These are the times that everything is a challenge to achieve, those times in which we believe all is in opposition to our interests or our well-being. we feel overwhelmed and do not know how to begin by

exit...

Do you have a spot? ... Good! Create a mind-map and then take the time to extend it...

Find the triggers that lead you to lose motivation.

What are the reasons to set goals?

When we drive our vehicle and go either to the left or right? We believe that we will arrive in time? What can we do to ensure that we have enough fuel? Why do we wear a tie in this moment?

It is likely because we know who we'll meet and that we are in a position to see the distance we stand from our place of meeting and we have a clear title of the town, or the district.

It is also possible to think that the purpose of this meeting is meaningful to us and matches with the Nietzschean " what " as a rationale to justify of what it signifies to us.

In terms of " how "it is connected with "sense" to indicate direction or orientation.

In short, we create a target for ourselves.

Setting goals is about giving yourself something to think about! It is determining what we'd like to achieve and the best routes and resources that will help us to achieve it.

For employees of the company, the main goals are

" Fixes" by the top management or shareholders, they are not often changeable. On the other hand the methods and ways that we achieve them are in our control. It's a matter of paying attention to"the "how," while knowing that we'll have everything to gain from being aware of the advantages of these goals, i.e., the "why." Our actions will be more fair and harmonious since we'll know the meaning behind them.

How do you define freedom? !

It is clear that the work done by Victor Frankl is a real source of inspiration to those who are unsure of the meaning of freedom. As a former survivor of prison camps, his traumatic suffering of poverty helped him define the concept that is that is dear to us all.

In this context, he said that mental health is built on a certain level of conflict between things we've done and what's left to be accomplished. The man's goal isn't to relax, but to work toward a definite purpose, to accomplish the task that he has chosen to do.

In this way it is believed that Buddha was questioned from one of his followers regarding how to live a life that was most enjoyable. The Buddha recognized that the man was musician. He asked him this question :

" How can you ensure that your zither produces the most effective tone?". " The pupil replied: "the strings should be not too tight or too loose." The Buddha then instructed him to draw his the inspiration of his experience regarding an instrument to live a life that is right.

Why do I have to break my head, and not accept the life in its entirety?

What happens when we stop doing anything? If we don't have any desire? It's then simpler to talk about the outcomes of our issues rather than discussing the best way to resolve them.

This is why it's not the inertia path we propose, instead, but one that helps us recognize our potential to take action in our daily lives to be able to give appropriate answers to our desire to develop.

In order to do this, some initial efforts are required, just as every time it comes to the issue of responsibility.

But where do I begin?

We would like to help you clarify some basic questions we have a way to avoid. We will provide brief and simple answers:
What do we really need?
What time do you need to achieve it?
* What can we afford to sacrifice for this?
What will be the one thing we will never give up?

It requires courage to tackle these questions since they'll bring us to our limitations and limitations as well as negative effects that can result from our goals.

Be sure to take the time to respond to your questions, and you will feel the sense of being in control of ourselves, and feeling at the helm of our life and we will think twice before accepting help, which often serves different needs than our own.

After having clarified my goals Should I pursue them head-on?

Now let's look up. What do we notice? Others! On the streets, at the work place, or at home, we're not on our own. We are in a shared social and cultural environment that we share with others in the vicinity.

Understanding our goal in context allows us to make it more palatable to our surroundings. It also lets us anticipate obstacles that could arise and to identify potential resources.

" My issue is time. ..."

Every day is a total in the form of 24 hour. There is no alternative but to invest it or spend it. By setting goals efficiently we execute an essential time management task which determines the effectiveness and consistency of all of our actions.

To reduce time, it is necessary to put it into.

The reason the goal is an issue in the company?

It is evident that we favor the reasoning of a firefighter who is called in to put out an blaze in a poorly constructed structure to the architect who is able to already caused the catastrophe when he designs his plans. We are in a type of survival position.

Under constant pressure, we tend to choose actions over reflection. This is often being absorbed into "unproductive" times. Furthermore, emergency care results in rapid satisfaction and consequently, satisfaction in getting an immediate result.

Perhaps it's the right time to tap into our capacity for anticipatory and proactiveness by distinguishing what is urgent and crucial ...

The predominant left brain

The tools suggested to tackle the problem are usually analytical and quantitative (left brain) such as spreadsheets, histograms diagram, matrix...

However, concepts like globality, vision, and visualization (right brain) are crucial to comprehend the purpose.

How do it?

We will review the basic principles that enable effectiveness in the formulation of goals.

When you are specific and concrete, as well as observable and quantifiable, the goal gains in precision and clarity. Rich is not a clear concept. A salary of EUR

100,000 over two years helps think about what needs to be accomplished.

The right brain doesn't recognize how to interpret the negative. This is what allows us to imagine our goals. The repeated statement "Tomorrow I'm not going to delay," won't be enough to make us more resourceful. In order to bring about a genuine change, we should use "tomorrow I'll be there by 8:15 am in the office " and the form that is stated is more effective for our purposes. Furthermore, it makes us to state what we want , and not what we do not would like to hear.

Similar to that, if we're instructed not to think of the image of a penguin on an iceberg wearing a mask and snorkel There is a high possibility that the image will come to dominate us in the end.

Let's think about whether the fulfillment of our goals is within our zone of influence; if not it's going to require negotiations or constant surveillance. "Being the top" is a mere wish beyond our influence since we don't constantly know who our rivals are or what they are making. However, "exceeding our turnover by 20 percent" is a goal of performance that depends on the control zone.

Let us imagine ourselves in the scenario where our goal is achieved. How do we feel? What are we trying to say? What are we seeing? The sensory projection creates an energizing loop in our present and helps to mobilize the power of all of our sources. It's a true body-feeling-spirit preparation that is extremely energetic.

It is a given that our goals must be in sync with our beliefs, our ultimate objective for our life (meta-objective). In the absence of this, we risk any chance of success. We'll always be in conflict within conscious, and most of all, not conscious. Our strategies is always thwarted as well as our attempts to be exhausted us. All of this will lead to the state of being unwell.

The context we place our goal in helps us verify its authenticity and coherence. It's a matter of identifying the individuals involved and the setting that it is taking place in.

If we are able to anticipate all outcomes that will result from reaching the goal (personal professional, family or community, etc.) Then, we are able to take care of the results ahead of time, instead of just waiting around for the consequences to happen.

Let us consider an apartment that matches the things we've always wanted in terms of size, surface as well as brightness, bedrooms, display... Is it willing to part with our child's nanny to give them to another person? Are we prepared to increase our travel time to work? There are many more questions we'll have to address prior to making commitments.

This holistic approach can save us from a number of issues. It will be implemented all the way through our journey, taking into consideration changing circumstances.

We must be clear in assessing the challenges and resources available, and then think of ways to overcome the former and determine and get rid of the resources.

We should set up indicators for the success. This will let us know when the goal was achieved.

The branches are able to provide the information they provide at this level, which is in response to "I will have achieved my goal when ...". The indicators must be tangible and frequently quantifiable.

A schedule is definitely essential and can take the form of retro-planning, which is, beginning from the date that is planned to achieve the aim to be lowered in successive phases until it finally reaches the exact date of the initial action to be undertaken.

It is believed that the first step, you must have already travelled half the distance. The act of taking action often removes fear.

As a good sailor we will keep our eyes in the direction of our goal, but always with an incredibly flexible and sense of possibility. Like the sailor, we will be sure to enjoy the final stages and finish with respect. We will gain new enthusiasm from this celebration and set out for new goals.

The mind map is a useful strategic tool

We'd like to present to you a method to utilize the objective-focused mind map. Maybe you'll use it in its current form or modify it to meet your needs, or discover other ways who are more in tune with your work. Most important is feeling at ease in your work and to have an underlying sense of control and in particular, not to feel unhelpful when faced with an unfinished page.

We suggest here a practical application of the heuristic map that follows the principles established in the past.

The process of creating maps provides us with to create a rational, sensory and a visionary visualization of our goals.

The appropriation of the goal through a body-mind-spirit approach, produces a high drive and creates a state of calm and continuous tension.

In this regard, we'll use an example of Chris is a sales executive at a life insurance company seeking to become more efficient in his work due to the new targets that were given to Chris in terms of turnover.

Be clear on the purpose

Chris realizes that he needs to first establish his goals. He creates the first map that has two branches. One is a representation of what he no longer desires and the other is the one that reflects what he would like to achieve.

The particular concrete, observable and quantifiable aspect will be regarded in both branches.

In the future every branch will be assigned a number which will enable Chris to determine whether or not within his control.

In relying on the things Chris no longer desires, Chris finds more easily what he truly desires. Chris can then identify the signs that he is successful.

The ramify

Chris will then be able to expand the ideas he has thought of in his dreams through the image of what he'll feel when he gets the objects.

The effectiveness of this work rests on the ability of the artist to create an evocation of a future state within his mind, as well as in his bodydue to the emotions he is in a position to create.

Drawings and words can trigger emotions, emotions, behavior ... In this moment, what needs to be the central point for the world map is likely to appear from its own. From him, you just look for a beginning and an idea. This is where the seed of all the implications.

Check

It's a matter of making sure that the goal and the route that is likely to achieve it are in harmony with the beliefs of Chris and the environment in which it operates.

In this way, the initial -level branches "respect" is divided into the second level "values" that Chris doesn't compromise. The consequences reflect the results of Chris's actions and the tangible consequences that result from the respect Chris has for his values.

The second part that is part of the 2nd level dedicated to the "environment" of Chris. The implications of the ramifications draw attention to the place within which Chris is located and the goal he has set by answering the questions: Where and with who?

The expectations relating to the results of the accomplishment of its goals regarding people as well as the environment are subject to consequences.

Two new branches at the first level can discern the required resources (third branch) and the probable difficulties (fourth branch). The implications of this permit Chris to design the best strategies to use the resources, and avoid or anticipate obstacles. Chris's keenness to stay on top of things leads to continuous updates to this particular branch.

The fifth branch of the first level is dedicated to the task of distributing tasks. The branch that is the same is named after the date Chris decided to achieve his goal or that forced upon him by his supervisors.

Each ramification outlines details of the work to be completed, its timeframe, the individuals who are involved, as well as the resources required to complete the task. Chris can mark, check out, or mark off after he has completed the task.

Sixth, first-level branches lets Chris to gather the different situations or data that may alter the strategy. This will help him keep a notes of the events which can be helpful for his case when he has to return for his hierarchy. Recollecting the story of these events helps remind him of the significance (the reason and the method) of his act.

On the seventh branch of the first level Chris determines ahead of time the rewards he'll award himself or will earn as he grows. The branch that Chris is considering as by Chris to be as crucial as the other branches because it permits him to get energy out of it. This is due to the reality that the information it carries is the most clear at the level of sensory perception (colors volumes, colors relief, emotions, etc.).

Heuristic map with value-added

Although we've arranged the stages of the user manual to ensure the sake of clarity in the demonstration, each branch could be separated from one other based on the amount of the information it needs to include. Maps are easily modified, by taking out or adding the ramifications.

We suggest keeping all cards that are produced for the same reason. This lets us review the progress we have made and evaluate the progress made.

The global perspective of all the parts of our map allows us to recognize the priority and the interdependence of various actions more quickly.

The more vivid, visual and clearly outlined maps are, the more easy it is to activate the anchors, thereby generating the desire to achieve the goal.

When we consider the usage of the map in times of being lost the mind map offers its users with clarity and peace that helps us keep a calm, regardless of the unexpected and varying stress.

Variations in the method

A goal may be a collective goal. In this instance the process remains the same. We recommend inviting everyone to make cards prior to the event. A facilitator then brings all of the cards into one, and encourages dialogue and listening between the participants.

Additionally, using the mind map as a part of coaching allows you to work on the information from prior sessions as well as for the preparation of the subsequent interviews. In this case an exact copy of the map is given to the coach as well as the coachee following each appointment.

Chapter 4: Mind Mapping Software

The Mind Mapping Principles program
When you're writing a job or are looking to improve your planning for business, these software can be extremely useful for you. The program provides an interface with visuals that can improve the entire process of writing from the beginning to the end. Mind mapping software allows you to organize your thoughts with the capability to increase or arrange them in a way that will enhance your experience. Increased productivity and accuracy is only one of the benefits this program offers, which can save you time and money for projects.

Mind mapping software allows your thoughts are displayed and you'll be able to see possible gaps or solutions to your ideas that can be filled in with fresh information. It's a great way to think creatively and solve issues with great accuracy. When your brain generates ideas it allows it to be recorded to allow you to view it all in one place.

It is easy to connect your thoughts to the software , and then begin changing them around and expanding the size of your thoughts to the maximum extent. This lets you see possible conflicts and provides you with the tools needed to identify and tackle the issues in your business plan or in writing assignments.

The majority of people who advocate mind mapping programs make use of the phrase "you might be able to see the forest and trees exactly at the same simultaneously". The interface lets you zoom out and see the entire concept as well as letting you get into the tiniest specifics and allowing you to go into detail about them. It can assist you to see and envision possibilities that would otherwise have been missed.

Time scheduling is an important benefit of brain mapping software since it allows you to identify the best tools to the tasks to be completed. When you're capable of observing the project and its phases clearly you can keep track of the percentage of work completed and make adjustments to ensure that the project is in line with time and budget. As a tool for management it can help you stay in a more efficient manner than ever before and help keep the production running.

While you work on your ideas on your own, you may utilize not only written words but also visual information to enhance your writing concepts. The majority of programs allow you to develop a variety of methods to organize information in various formats. You can use the data you generate to create jobs and make more informed decisions regarding these concepts.

Being a great problem solver is a concept centered on the brain mapping software. When you expand and organize your ideas to come to a sensible conclusion, you'll be able to beat the overwhelm of information and keep all of your information in a manner that could be modified instead of being lost. If you're the owner of an enterprise or manager the tools and resources included in applications are designed to aid you in getting the most efficiency in your projects from start to the end.

Every idea or new concept can be quickly expanded using an application for mind mapping. Many software companies offer trial versions , or even a no-cost standard software download that is located on their websites. Some offer more features than other companies, however they all share a few things in common: they are able to help you improve productivity and control of time.

The most effective mind mapping program The use of mind mapping software is getting more well-known as their benefits to business processes as well as brainstorming, project planning and creative writing are becoming more well-known. It is also, due to the rising popularity, so is the effort and care involved in the creation and development of mind mapping software and tools.

Because a good mind mapping software can cost hundreds of dollars for an individual user, it's essential to select the right one for your needs. In this article I'll go over two recommended programs that I'm sure will meet your needs to the fullest and provide you with an excellent user experience.

The software is compatible with the Mac and Windows platforms and offers a great amount of value to consumers. I think they could provide an impressive ROI for the company you're in.

There are many reasons to use software for mind mapping

The Mind Mapping software program is the most efficient method of increasing efficiency , in addition to writing the necessary records for your little business's activities or writing tasks. The software for computers is miles ahead of the old-fashioned pencil and paper method of working. It's an innovative and modern method of getting the job completed quickly. Here are 10 benefits to utilize a mind mapping application.

Mind mapping software are beneficial to your company. Computer software can be used help you improve your thinking and assist you in becoming an improved visual-

oriented in your management of theories and as a problem-solver for your boss. The time spent on projects from start to finish is likely to be seen by all.

Another advantage is that it's an adaptive software that is able to adapt to changing circumstances. The Mind Map software can be flexible , as it allows users to alter their your thoughts and come up with solutions quickly. While you develop your thoughts, it offers you the capability to choose the right tools to help you get the job completed faster.

It allows you to find holes. One of the most beneficial aspects of this computer program is that it allows users to discover holes in the thinking process, meaning that you can visualize the issue and create an alternative plan of action.

Mind mapping software brings powerful tools at your fingertips. If you create a subject and then move it around your port, you organize it and then re-evaluate it in an abstract way so that you are able to think about your concept from every angle. This lets you create solutions in a short time.

Learn to create marketing strategies. Another excellent tool for your plan is to create complete and efficient strategies for marketing and advertising with a visual layout so you can expand or reduce your thoughts easily.

Mind mapping software helps simplify your business. After you've grasped the basic principles of the program and you're able to utilize it to determine the appropriate amount of action to every task. You are able to apply only the appropriate amount of human power and other equipment needed to complete the task. You can manage the speed of your project by using the built-in clock. This allows you to remain up-to-date with your schedule goals. It's possible to view the big picture and great information immediately after using this application. The changing and expanding nature of the interface allows users to zoom into amazing depth to control the fine details or zoom to see the bigger picture of exactly what your goals are.

It allows you to track your assignments and projects. Once you've gotten your focus on your thoughts, you are able to focus on getting the tasks done and tracking the development each day. As you approach the end of your project It is possible to change the order and expand, or even create new possibilities to make your work done more efficiently or less costly. Clarity of thought. One of the most talked about characteristics of this computer program is its ability to eat the brainstorming ideas you have created and instantly sort them out to explain the concept. Mind mapping software uses graphics and colour to improve memory. When you can get your thoughts visible in full-color or with images laid to be organized and arranged, it's will increase your capacity to solve all issues that may arise.

Top mistakes to avoid the mind mapping program

The Mind Mapping software can be a powerful instrument for today's information worker. It's a flexible tool to plan and grow your business. Because of its flexibility inherent - its method of operation "encapsulates" information and thoughts, meaning it is able to be easily altered or rearranged, and annotated - there is nothing better than a carefully designed visual map when it comes to the communication of ideas and creating an understanding of the idea.

But, as with the majority of productivity software mind mapping programs are a weapon that is a myth. It could also be used to create vague ideas and mislead others. Worse, visually mapped maps that are poorly designed can be used to take an open-minded or left-brained person and completely turn them off to the idea of representing information and ideas visually.

To make sure your mind maps don't belong in this category Here are 10 mistakes to avoid using software for mind mapping to create visual maps for your work:

1. Avoid putting excessive detail within your mental maps. It's easy to create topics with excessive levels of detail. This could create the visual "clutter" and may cause confusion to others in the event that you are discussing your maps in a group discussion.

2. Don't be erratic in the use of colors shapes, shapes, line styles and other visual elements in your maps. Each one can aid in conveying a deeper meaning or context, if utilized consistently and in a systematic manner. When used arbitrarily, they can create confusion.

3. Be careful not to have too much text about your subjects. Make use of specific keywords and phrases to draw people into the flow that is your road map. Be sure to keep your subject's names concise 1- 3 words maximum. If you'd like to include more details make use of your application's "notes" function to store the details. It can be hidden from the view of

your users, thus reducing visual clutter and making it just a mouse tap away.

4. Do not ignore your app's symbol or icons. They are often used to classify your map's contents visually, and are helpful if you have to filter the contents of a large map.

5. Beware of over-use for visual maps. As with all things, it's likely to push your brain mapping software to the extreme, and even use it to help you make your shopping lists.

6. Do not make one map with everything insideit, since it's likely to rapidly become uncontrollable. Instead, use the program's capabilities to create sub-maps, which are connected maps that make it easier to comprehend and manage.

7. Do not just make mind maps that are based on text. To get the most advantage from using visual maps ensure that you include pictures in your maps. This will help them in appealing to either part of your brain.

8. Prevent "map jolt". The audience may be overwhelmed when they see an

intricate visual map , and might suffer from "map Jolt". Consider presenting information in both linear and mapped formats to ensure that you don't overwhelm your audience.

9. Beware of the conventional wisdom that mapping is all about inspiration and creativity. It's actually more. It's an extremely efficient tool to manage data overload in the creation and execution of projects, and making better decisions and has many other benefits for businesses!

10. Do not reinvent the wheel. Search the web as well as in books for most effective techniques.

We'll start by introducing the basic concept first. Mind maps are an illustration of the process of thinking as it's a graphic representation. it's visually stimulating and it allows you to see the connection between the main subjects and the details branches. For someone with an excellent eye Mind maps are a great choice for me. Mind mapping software excels in this way because it's easy to create maps and add images with a fantastic software.

What do you think about using mind maps applications to tap into the auditory learning process? The first option you could consider doing while you design your map would be to talk to yourself with a gentle voice, explaining your actions in the manner you're able. While this may assist, another useful feature of mind mapping apps is the capability to add audio files . This means that you can create your own division and save your thoughts on the division for you to listen to at a later time. Let me move ahead a bit and recommend you use the imindmap application because of this. Other programs allow users to connect to audio files, however you'll need to create connections in a separate app and connect to it and once you're ready to play the file, you will need to open your default MP3 player. But, imindmap has this cool feature called sound notes which allows you to record the note within the program (you only need a microphone) and then connect directly into the division.

Then, we go back to the learning through kinesthetic. When you draw maps with a hand-drawn design the physical act of drawing the branch at a particular location on the map is a tap into the learning mode. The direction of the branch, its width and the physical act of using an alternative colored pencil contribute to the physical experience. The first attempts to create mind maps were limited by their physical interaction with the map as it was merely a matter of inserting the key in your computer to generate the new branch or basic stage, and clicking actions using the mouse.

Most current software programs aren't able to do this, but one of the reasons imindmap is moving forward is because it's managed to reproduce the physical activity of this hand-drawn procedure using a computer. This is a huge benefit to individuals and women who possess an advantage in the way that they process and process information.

Chapter 5: Mind Mapping Tools

Pen And Paper vs. The Computer What are the Advantages And Minuses?

Mind mapping can be a useful method of boosting your creative abilities and organizing your thoughts. But what tools do you use to map?

There are two primary methods to utilize mind tools for mapping.

You can utilize the old stylus and paper processes or use the new computer system.

This book outlines both benefits and drawbacks.

At first, I begin using a pen and a piece of paper, before I move on to software to map.

Pen and paper This generally is done with an unlined white piece of paper and colored designs.

Advantage.

1. It's fairly inexpensive. Paper and pen are affordable all over the world.
2. There is no need to know the program.

Advantages

1. It's easy to look sloppy and unprofessional, if you're not an artist of high quality and spending the time to create it correctly.

2. It's difficult to make a post. If you're looking to alter the branch's location it is possible to rebuild the entire mental map.

3. Most of the time, you're getting a little overwhelmed. It is likely that you will end to the other side of the screen when you are looking to relax your mind.

You could try to use bigger sheets of paper but they isn't able to handle.

Computer Software

It's a recent advancement, and is the direction the mind mapping process is clearly headed appears to be.

Advantage

1. It's professional looking. You don't need to be a genius or understand how to arrange the parts. You'll be confident and confident should you decide to share your secrets with anyone.

2. Editing is simple.

You can adjust the divisions and the information you write on them.

It is particularly helpful in the event that you can coordinate your thoughts following a successful brainstorming session.

3. The documents and reports are connected to divisions. It is a distinct part.

It provides another dimension to the maps of your brain.

There are shortcuts you can make on your mind map that will take you to your associated files and sites.

4. You'll be able to create superior mind mappings. The paper's bottom doesn't restrict you.

It is possible to play. This ensures that your imagination and feelings don't have a limit.

5. It is possible to transform a division into single map hub. It will help you concentrate on a particular subtopic and generate a variety of ideas.

Disadvantage.

1. You'll be learning a new software. It includes everything from mind mapping

applications to software to create charts and graphs, so you need to find the appropriate software to use for these.

2. It requires money to buy.

I'm talking about, but also do many positive things in the present. I realise. The investment was worthwhile for me. I use it regularly which has greatly improved.

Analyzing, both have their advantages and disadvantages, however, I prefer apps for myself due to the benefits mentioned above.

I'd like to know about certain benefits of technology are not included in some products for mind mapping.

My blog for more details on the mind map software.

When it comes to maps are concerned, I was once thinking of a map on paper, but I now think of a computer-generated map.

Everyone of us will eventually have certain interests. It is our responsibility to choose.

Happily mapping your mind! Enjoy mind mapping!

Mind Map Software

Mind mapping is a fun exercise that starts with the writing of the main idea or topic before drawing lines to connect them to different "nodes," each of them with a different concept or word that is connected to the initial.

It's easy enough.

If you're left with an unfinished piece of paper that is on the globe, but using a digital method makes the process easy and versatile.

There are no limits in the dimension of your piece of paper using a digital mental map that can rapidly change thoughts with minimal effort.

We've reviewed a variety of mind mapping tools We have selected the top 11 devices to help you figure out the most effective method to chart your thoughts.

What is it that makes software for Great Mind Mapping?

Each of the top mind mapping tools have distinct advantages, but they all offer the following benefits: Linen is free.

If you aren't able to stretch your mind's mapping the canvas, it could be restricted because you are running into space.

If you aren't able to see the whole map at once it is possible to imagine an endless map until you've finished.

Capable of attaching documents.

Sometimes the words aren't enough to convey your thoughts, or perhaps you require an additional document to use in your sketching.

You can attach images, links and other documents in your map with all the top mind mapping applications.

The characteristics of collaboration

Mind mapping applications that are that are cloud-based can facilitate collaboration and comments on the canvas for multiple users.

The top desktop apps allow for ample sharing and the syncing of cloud-based data between platforms, so that many users have use the data and refresh their mind map.

Exporting and saving. These apps permit you to save and edit your map at any time as well as the capability of sharing maps or exporting them online.

What's inside

It's futuristic, and perhaps scary, especially when you are done introducing the word technology.

The Mind Mapping software.

It suggests that the mysterious human brain will reside in the brain's deep regions.

Perhaps for reasons of danger.

It could also be an excellent sci-fi movie!

Mind mapping isn't as scary, in fact the majority of people realize that this is just the method they're using to grasp the subject that they want to master.

It's the act of organizing the many information elements within your mind, in an unlinear fashion that allows you to see connections between objects even when the relationships were not always evident.

Mind mapping allows individuals within their minds to enter an application on a computer where software transforms it into an visualization that lets people see everything simultaneously.

What exactly is a mindmap exactly?

Visual charts are just sketch. It is able to depict anything, and is often used to chart diagrams

Concepts

Ideas

Aims

Tasks

Emotions

Problems/Solutions

or team building activities , or individual and creative activities.

A consultant could be able to, for instance, ask an individual buyer to develop an image of the word 'fear, or a boss may request the employee to develop an inner plan of action around the phrase 'profits increased.

It is a well-known method of brainstorming and is very interesting for those who do not perform their work linearly.

Software for mind mapping can aid to make mind mapping a lot easier. Utilizing software has numerous advantages over doing it manually.

More Options.

This program can create drawings in ways that you would never have imagined, yet it can be useful to you. Colors, shapes contacts, and storage of other materials all contribute to your mind diagram.

3-D.

It's the latest advancement of the maps. If thinking isn't linear Why should be two-dimensional?

More memory.

Computers are able to remember more than you do therefore more thoughts is able to be absorbed into your head. It drastically decreases the likelihood that you'll look at your forehead thinking, I'm sorry!" Mind mapping software can organize and give easy access to more information than human brains can wrap itself around.

An entire information network.

There are documents, links, records attachments, visuals and other information using Mind Mapping that you could never imagine.

Mind mapping is a quaint idea, but the technology to map your mind takes it into the 21st century.

Utilizing this technique it is possible to visualize the possibilities, plan the coordinates, discover how to analyse, plan and see more possibilities than you would.

It's a valuable tool anyone can use, and obviously having more tools means more and more efficient.

What is the reason Mind Mapping Software Beats Paper

What is the reason Mind Mapping Software Beats Paper

The concept to map your mind has been around for a long time. In actuality, the mind maps are sketched dating back to the 3rd century. porphyry from Tyros.

In the 60s Allan M. Collins and M made the first mind map. Ross Quillian. Because of the mind mapping software that have further developed, they are even more advanced even in 2009.

Instead of paper-based versions The use of mind mapping software provides a variety of advantages.

When you draw an abstract diagram on paper, there's no way to change the order of concepts without editing them manually and writing them over again or creating an entirely new diagram.

You can organize your thoughts multiple times using mind mapping software until they're in the exact place you'd like them to be. This saves you lots of stress and frustration.

Another benefit of mind mapping applications is the ability to store concepts in collapsible tree forms that you can expand as required.

Mind maps that are drawn on paper don't provide this flexibility and, in the end they appear extremely disorganized and chaotic.

There's no limit to the amount of information you can put into the topic trees that can be collapsible with the program.

It could contain Word as well as Excel documents, hyperlinks to websites, e-mails lists, etc.

It also reduces the amount of paperwork to be completed by the client.

Everything is available on the online mind map. All it takes is a click away. What a huge benefit!

You can also export ideas and the information into other applications using the mind map tools if needed.

It allows you to create diagrams for any project by prioritising and organizing the information prior to it being vitally important to use applications such as display and project management, or word processing applications.

You can also send the chart to team members so that they can download it and then add their own data.

In addition, this program allows you to showcase your concepts to a crowd of people simultaneously using an LCD projector as well as a screen.

Although it is similar to PowerPoint however, it's not exactly the same because mind mapping software lets users to add data quickly and instantly on your graph in real-time throughout meetings and brainstorming sessions.

PowerPoint presentations don't offer this necessary flexibility.

The benefits of using mind mapping applications aren't limited to those mentioned above.

There are many other advantages that are waiting to be found. The flexibility of the mind map tools have led to numerous applications of mind maps, including the development of a business strategy, management of projects to the monitoring of your personal goals , and writing books.

Mind mapping software helps with the organization for your ideas, thoughts for almost every upcoming project or event , and can help you save time and energy at a central location.

Mind Mapping Software Helps Personal Development

It's no fact that mapping your mind can be used for numerous practical and business-related applications, however, fewer realize that it could be an enormous help to personal growth.

In the personal life Mind mapping software can aid people.

It helps them organize and arrange items around them, like schedules, calendars , and things like thoughts, feelings and even memories.

Here's a few examples of mind mapping apps that can help you improve your skills.

Control Of Time.

The flow of time seems to be in a linear manner, but that doesn't mean that our goals will automatically will be achieved.

Mind maps software can help us determine what tasks we need to be done, who's in charge and how we can keep our time in order to ensure our families get the most effective outcomes.

Memories.

Sometimes it seems as if memories are gone, but usually, they're somewhere in the depths of the ocean. Mind maps can help you develop websites that share similar ideas and feelings.

Making Choices.

The majority of institutions and businesses use concept mapping software, however family members and friends can also use it, too.

With this program, every option and its potential outcomes can be mapped quickly and clearly. It's also a great method for teaching children to make difficult decisions during their daily lives.

Question Management.

Mind maps can assist you to change from a situation where you respond to problems to a position that you can change your situation by thinking creatively. Through the use of mind mapping tools the more ideas will become clear.

Emotional Health.

The majority of clinicians use mental visualization techniques to assist patients understand their feelings however, you can also apply it to yourself too.

You're unhappy, angry and discontent? Make a map of your thoughts and you'll discover some new perspectives that could delight you.

Create The Target.

It may seem like an easy process that follows D, as you go through steps A,B and C, but many different methods are available to discover and set goals that linear thinking isn't capable of revealing.

Once you have gotten your ideas in your head, using the mapping program, innovative possibilities and opportunities are numerous possibilities.

Spiritual Development.

Mind mapping can help obviously, to discover your values in the spiritual realm and objectives However, it could be more than that.

Mind maps are an expression of meditation or even medicine. By using this technique you can contemplate the nature or purpose of your higher self.

It's helpful to worship each aspect of God's persona as it unfolds within your mind's depths.

It can be challenging to meditate for those who are prone to fumbling around in silence However, if your mind is able to relax through recording your thoughts, you are able to float along spiritual paths for free.

Anxiety, or unjust treatment.

Sometimes, it's a way to vent all the negative emotions. Make use of your mind mapping software and write them down to take an inhalation before hitting on delete. See.

Go! This is the only thing that can make you feel fearful.

The usage of mind maps, mental mapping and even brain maps is almost infinite.

Spend some time learning the ways this unique and reliable tool can improve your quality of life.

Chapter 6: The Benefits Of Mind Mapping

Mind mapping improves memory

The process of mind mapping is an unique mix of visual spatial arrangement imagery and color. It has been proven to significantly improve recall, opposed to the traditional method of learning through rote learning and note-taking.

Mind mapping can boost creativity

Mind maps assist in increasing creativity and also enabling users to come up with fresh ideas when you brainstorm. The spatial layout allows you to gain a greater view of the situation, and also allows you to easily identify new connections to generate endless thoughts connections, associations, and thoughts on any subject.

Mind mapping can help in learning

Research has proven that the mind mapping techniques are an extremely effective tool for teaching. It increases the visual appeal of a subject through the use of symbols, images and colors, and assists students to make sense of concepts by creating ideas in sensible ways. This method is great for stimulating active learning, increasing confidence, encouraging motivation as well as encouraging a variety of skills and learning techniques.

Mind mapping can be used to support effective teaching

Mind mapping can be regarded as a pedagogical instrument that is visible and provides an effective way to encourage more understanding among students. It's also adaptable and can provide a wide range of applications within the school setting.

Mind mapping enhances presentation skills

A study that looked into the benefits of mind mapping has revealed that many students were able to create clear and persuasive presentations with just a sketch of their mind maps, without shuffles around with notes. Students found it easier to tackle difficult questions. The students' ability to communicate information in a way that was effective could be traced back to improved recall of data, as it was retained as well as stored in a more complex radiating fashion instead of linearly. Students were able better to comprehend the information better since they had a personal representation of the data.

Mind mapping can help facilitate group collaboration

Mind mapping is a fantastic way to work with other people in the process of implementing major projects or creating plans. It lets you utilize everyone's input in a dynamic and creative method. You can write down all thoughts or statements in your Mind Map and then talk about them at the right moment.

Mind mapping can improve writing abilities

Mind maps are an excellent tool to enhance any type of writing. It assists you in getting all the important information and thoughts down and arrange them in meaningful ways simultaneously. Writing is then a simple task of reading your mind map, then creating a paragraph or a sentence on each crucial word.

Mind mapping encourages problem solving and critical thinking

A mind map can allow the mind to focus more to understand the connections between ideas and elements of an argument, and also to think of solutions to issues. It provides a fresh perspective, aiding you in identifying the most important issues and then evaluating your options relative to the overall picture. It makes it simpler to organize information in a systematic manner and incorporate new knowledge because you're not tied to a fixed structure.

Uses of Mind Mapping

Before you can begin to learn the methods used in mind mapping, and how you can apply them to your daily life it is crucial to be aware of its benefits. Many writers use this technique when they experience writer's block, or they are having difficulty organizing thoughts or ideas. Here are some uses of mind mapping:

*Taking meeting notes

Notes using the mind map is a fantastic way to document the ideas that are discussed during a meeting. This is particularly so because meetings are generally non-linear, and seldom do they have any specific agenda. Most of the time, meetings usually involve the discussions of ideas, information exchange and the discussion of numerous thoughtsthat require to be documented. The text notes can be considered to be linear and that makes it challenging to record ideas that are discussed in meetings in a timely manner, especially when the meeting is not linear.

*Book summary

Mind maps are particularly efficient when it comes to creating summary of books. Non-fiction books, in particular contain concepts and ideas which you should be able to record while reading. If you are a lover of reading and usually make notes while reading you read, you might have felt the desire to write an additional idea to an idea you've been pondering on a different page. Maybe you want to look up notes from earlier ones to establish a connection. This can be particularly difficult when you're using texts, and the concepts can result in many messy notes. Mind maps are excellent to summarize information, similar to the ones is found in books. It is possible to create concepts and ideas by using branches to illustrate the most important concepts in notes. You can also make them easier to understand.

*Project management

There are a variety of tools and software programs for the task of managing projects, you can also use mind maps to organize and manage smaller projects. Start by having your primary idea portrayed as the primary project, then you can have the following branches created:

Budget

People

Deadline

Resources

Scope

These branches are the core of every project. This is why it is easy to create an outline of your mind to oversee your project. Once you have set up these branches, you are able to check them out frequently as you progress with the project.

*Studying

Mind maps can be useful especially while studying. You can utilize them for two different purposes to take notes during lectures as well as when you are studying; and secondly connecting the dots while preparing for tests and exams. If you have a mental map of the information you wish to remember, you can effortlessly connect the dots by using your mindmap to grasp the content at a fundamental level. Therefore, you'll realize that you do not require the minute details to grasp the idea. Once you've grasped the fundamental concepts and the strokes that you are able to easily apply the concepts (of course it takes practice) and solve issues like effortless.

* Goal setting

Everyone has goals at some moment in their lives. Similar to the majority of people, you use a the pen and paper to note on your list of goals. It's not an unwise choice. In fact, this strategy has been in use for centuries and has proved successful for a lot of people. However, there's an alternative method to set your goals: with mind maps. The main reason you should make use of mind maps for setting goals is because they're memorable. Why? Because they employ visualization by using diagrams and images. When you write your goals on paper and you are able to visualize the results in your mind. The ability to visualize your goals while setting them is essential in their execution and that is the reason why mind maps are far more efficient than notes on paper.

*Problem resolution

Different approaches can be used for problem solving, but one excellent method to employ is the outline 5W and 1H that you use to ask yourself a few questions that must be answered, specifically:

Who

Where are you?

How do I
What is it?
When

This is an excellent use of mind maps because when you go through each of the sections, chances are good that you'll discover connections between your responses. These are easily located in the mind map. When you have answers to these questions, you'll notice that the issue is becoming more clear, and will help to find a solution. Mind mapping can be used to resolve a problem, make your issue the primary idea and the issues to be depicted by branches. As much as you can to address these questions in a single step and, as you discover solutions to each of them, you'll probably find an answer.

*Brainstorming

The problem about the process of brainstorming is that it typically involves sharing a variety of ideas, and at times the majority of them might not be logical. This is why it is easy to record every thought in a mind map and then organize them later to create reasonable ideas. We'll go over more on this further.

Management

The majority of people use taking notes on paper when studying to better grasp a certain subject. It can be very inefficient often, especially when you're trying to remember something in the midst of a long paragraph of text. It's not ideal and tedious to read through these notes when you could make use of a mind map to find specific ideas regarding the subject. Instead of making notes to record data, make use of the mind map to bring information to your database. Knowledge management is quick and efficient, particularly nowadays with the advent of software-based mind maps. For instance, you could create an information bank about business networking. There are a lot of PDF documents that contain information, tips, notes in text on incredible books on business networking as well as a mind map about business networking using social media. What is the best method to create a knowledge bank by combining all the data in various formats and in various files? It is important to have all of this information centralized and linked together in one location. It is possible to represent the entire information in an omnipresent mind map which will serve like a knowledge database. You can manage the information by creating branches on mind maps that are organized in a way , and in a straightforward format that is simple to look over.

*Getting things completed

Mind maps are useful in providing information in a simple format for quick recall but they're certainly not as effective when creating the list of things to do. It is more likely that you benefit from paper and pen when it comes to this area. However, this doesn't suggest that you shouldn't utilize mental maps in order to help get work accomplished. They can prove extremely helpful, particularly when you utilize techniques for productivity like agile Results as well as when you map your GTD Horizons, then map them onto a mind map and then assign those tasks over to the task supervisor.

*Decision-making

When you face circumstances that require you to make an important decision, it best to have a range of choices to pick from. There are two options to choose from: of two choices that include paper and pen or even mind maps. All of these options involve drawing out your alternatives using paper, the main difference with minds maps lies in the fact that they visualize the choices to make it easy to follow-up. This can make a huge amount of difference, especially when you're weighing various alternatives. It is simple to recognize connections between options due to it's visual appeal. This is particularly true when you sketch the various scenarios, and it becomes much easier to connect the various alternatives to find the most suitable solution.

We'll go over the specific methods to use mind mapping in different aspects that you live in next chapters of this book. Before we begin, let's take a an overview of the various methods of mind mapping that you can employ to achieve success in different aspects of your life. Then we reduce it to particular areas in your life.

Chapter 7: Mind Mapping Examples

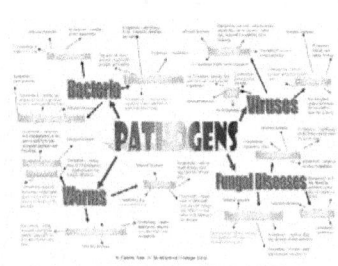

This chapter will be focusing on three common and utilized Mind Maps. Be aware that you're not limited to the examples given in the next section. Make use of these examples as a guide in designing Your own Mind Maps.

Mind Maps for students

If there was a particular category of people who would benefit most of Mind Mapping, I would say it's the students. If you're studying, it is likely that you'll find yourself attending hundreds of classes. Every lecture is filled with details. What's more important than having several of them in one day? In addition, there are the endless studies you must learn and the endless presentation that you must create and talk about. With all that is happening, it can be difficult for a student to become overwhelmed. A well-designed Mind Map will help him keep track of his goals and help him achieve his objectives in a timely fashion.

The Mind Maps for students can be useful to accomplish the following tasks:

Management of information

There are always assignments to complete. However, more than the writing of these papers the most challenging job for students is to organize and sort through the plethora of data that he's collected from his lectures and research. It's easy to write a good paper if you know what you want to write about. A Mind Map will assist a student develop a framework of way he wants his essay to be written. After that, he'll be able to simplify the details he needs and design them to the layout he constructed.

Exam preparation Exams

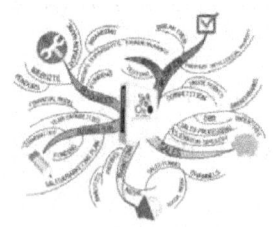

It's another gruelling task that many students hate. There's nothing more tedious and painful than reading the same text line after line and trying to learn the words. Mind Maps can help improve memorization. This map employs an ethereal or tree-like structure and is believed to reflect the way in which the brains store and retrieve information and data. Due to this, the mind is able to take notes from Mind Maps Mind Map instead of a book. Mind Maps also use catchy words, images and colors. These visual representations serve as triggers for memory which help the brain to recall them.
Notes!

Noting down notes can be a tedious assignment for learners. Mind Maps can make them an enjoyable process. The use of a tree-like diagram, color and images make writing notes more enjoyable.

Presentations

Reports and presentations are a essential task for students. The issue is how present the audience with an organized and clean version of all the information you've collected. Your presentation should be entertaining. Use of bullet points is sure to put your audience off. Your presentation needs to draw their attention.It should be fun but also informative. Mind Maps can do all this for you. You can use them on your presentation the actual Mind Map. It is also possible to create it on the Mind Map itself as you walk in your present. This will draw your audience a bit more with the topic you're talking about.

Daily check-list

In addition to your tests as well as your notes and reports there are many other tasks and errands that you must complete on a daily basis. Don't panic. Don't worry about it. The school experience is among the most rewarding experiences that a person could ever have. It's the perfect time to establish new friendships. It's the time to discover something new about yourself and your friends. Enjoy it. You can be studying and having enjoyable too. It's just a matter of making time for these activities. Make use of Mind Maps to help you keep track of your time.

Below is an example Mind Map of the student who is likely to be studying for an examination on Pathogens:

(Photo Credit:Here)

Mind mapping for business

The mind mapping technique can be extremely beneficial for businesses. It's a highly efficient and powerful tool that can be utilized to encourage collaboration between employees and team members. It will help enhance communication among departments and divisions. Employees are also more involved in the business's operations as they become in a position to comprehend the bigger overall picture, the structure and vision of the business and the goals it's trying achieve.

Since employees are able to take in the goals the company is trying encourage, productivity and productivity are improved. Instead of using graphs and charts to show the performance of employees and their productivity it is possible to simply show the concept of a Mind Map. This can create a presentation that is more engaging and informative, as well as more memorable.

Below is an example Mind Map of an owner of a business who is looking to launch his company:

Mind Mapping to Set Goals for Mind Maps
Everyone has ambitions and goals in our lives and we all hope to accomplish these goals. However, life happens. When we embark on our journey, we'll meet difficulties. A curve ball is likely to be thrown at us. If this happens and we are caught, we could be tempted to turn away from the roads that are meant to lead us

to our goals. What can we do? What can we do to return to our normal course?

Mind Mapping helps us keep our focus. When life doesn't seem to be gentle, it's a great way to be reminded visually of our objectives in life. The idea of having our goals displayed before our eyes will assist us in ensuring that we'll be right. We have alternatives and plans all planned out.

All we have to do is do to adhere to the guidelines. Mind Mapping can help us sort through the mess of our minds. While our thoughts are in peace and we are able to allow ourselves to remain still. When we're in a state of calm in a state of calm, we can discern clearly. We can pursue our goals with renewed enthusiasm and enthusiasm.

Below is an example Mind Map of one's goals in life:

Chapter 8: Benefits of Using Mind Maps

There are many advantages to making use of mind maps, regardless of the stage of your life or the things you do. They're an effective instrument that anybody can access and make use of to benefit themselves.

The main benefits of mind mapping is they represent how your brain perceives the world around you and make connections between various things. Mind maps can bring clarity to any decision-making or learning process by combining the various processes your brain employs in order to organize information.

When you're mind mapping it is making use of your entire brain to think.

The advantage of mind maps is that it allows you to quickly and quickly determine what are the most significant ideas based on the degree of proximity to the concept in the center, as well as by the way it's presented.

The connections between concepts can be observed quickly, allowing your brain to make connections between concepts. This makes it easier to study and master terms and the relationships rapidly since your brain can remember and visualize it quickly.

A mind map is extremely easy to develop. It is possible to easily add additional details along with concepts and ideas as you gain more about the topic. They're not static in any way They are a fluid way of expressing the information that you would like to store.

Mind maps create patterns using colours and shapes, which are what your brain is quite adept in remembering. Just visualizing the patterns in your map may aid in recalling the data. The visualisation helps your brain to make connections between the various concepts and bits of information you've recorded, assisting you put together this information , and create leaps of understanding.

Mind maps offer a variety of advantages, and even more than what's listed ones mentioned above. Like we said, they can be powerful instruments that aid you in understanding concepts, make informed decisions and understand information faster and less time-consuming way than traditional methods. A few of the areas that mind maps could be beneficial in the following areas:

Learning. Mind maps can help you feel comfortable learning and revising. They will increase confidence in your ability to learn and study for your exams.

Overviewing. When it comes to problem-solving or learning the ability to get an eye-to-eye view of the problem that are at hand is beneficial. Mind maps can help you discover the links and connections between different problems and allow you to make connections that you might have missed otherwise.

Concentration. Mind maps can help you concentrate on the task you are working on and utilize all your mental capabilities to pay focus. The mind map itself was created to draw your attention as well as assist in concentration.

Memorizing. Visual media can help you remember, since the majority of people respond well to visual stimuli. You are able to "see" the map of your brain through your eye, which aids in recall.

Organization. Mind maps are a fantastic method of organizing details for revisions and projects in addition to other things.

Presentations. Mind maps can be used to aid you in giving an effective presentation. You can keep your mind in the right direction and focused on the content you wish to share with your audience.

Brainstorming. Mind maps are a fantastic tool for brainstorming. They help you arrange your ideas and thoughts in a logical manner that is clear after the session is finished.

Problem-solving. If you're facing a challenge and need to solve it, you can put all the relevant information in the shape of a mindmap and utilize this in order to link the dots among the various pieces of information. This will enable you to think creatively and solve problems, and come up with solutions that you might not otherwise have.

Thinking. Sometimes, it is necessary to maintain clarity of mind Mind maps is a great tool to achieve this. Mind maps are a great way to record what you think and feel about any topic.

Summarizing books/seminars. A lot of people want to summarize seminars or books or mind-maps are an a fantastic method to accomplish this. It is possible to summarize the content and connect ideas and points to one another.

Planning. Mind maps can assist you in planning your event or project. They can be used to present data and ensure that all steps and events are recorded.

There are many benefits to making use of mind maps in your professional and personal life. Many people around the globe who regularly utilize mind maps and reap the benefits of their use. You can also profit from this effective technique that can assist you in studying better learn faster, perform better, and be successful in your work.

The Best Way to Create an Mind Map

There are many possible ways to create mind maps, but there's a specific set of symbols and a method for making an effective mind map that is followed, helps make the mind map more easy to comprehend and also for other people to be able to comprehend.

Before you begin you'll need pencils and pens. If you have colored ones, it will be useful. They can be bought in a local shop for only a couple of dollars. You'll also require paper. The paper has to be landscape-oriented (i.e. the longest edge is located at high). This will give you more room to sketch your map.

In the middle of the paper, you should write down the principal idea you're imagining. It should be placed in the middle so that all other things can be linked with it, and spread from this central spot. This visual method can be extremely useful in helping you retain and grasp the basic concepts.

If you are mapping your mind for an event or book or revising and you create the mindmap as you move along and are learning. If you're using mind mapping to resolve a problem it will take your mind more fluid and you'll need to record it without allowing your mind to take over. The mind map is drawn in a continuous manner until you've got everything down.

You can be as imaginative as you like using the mindmap you create. Some prefer using word boxes or boxes while others prefer using colors and pictures to create their mind maps. It's a personal choice and is based on your preferences. If you think the former is the best for you, go with this, however if you prefer the other choose this. There's no one right or wrong choice It's all about personal choice.

Sometimes, an image will be more effective because images are worth the words it says and lets you explore your imagination and other connections. Utilizing color is an excellent idea as it stimulates your brain and draws your interest. Be sure that your image is of a decent size since you have to be able see the image clearly and have enough space to add other ideas onto it.

Within this central image it is important to place the key points you intend to address. These are the words that have to be written in capital letters because they are crucial. They're like chapters in books. Connect them with the main image by using strong (or colored) curving links, similar to branches that connect on the tree's trunk. the tree.

The printing of these ideas in letters allows your brain to take pictures of the words, which helps you to remember it better. Try using one word whenever you can, because it is easier for your brain to remember the meaning of that. If you are using several words at once, make sure you do not divide it into separate lines as the line break can cause the words to be separated in your brain.

If you employ curving lines to connect these words to the main image, this creates an aesthetic flow to the drawing, which makes it more easy to remember and more pleasing to the eyes. By making the lines longer they are regarded as more significant that is recognized by the brain.

After that step is to add a second step on each branch. These are images or words that trigger concepts or give information. Words are printed, but you are able to make use of lower case instead of joined-up writing. The connecting lines should be shorter since they are farther in the distance from where the central line is.

Do not stress about completing the first branch before moving to the next one; you let the information flow effortlessly.

The smaller words as well as the smaller lines signify that they are farther from the center and are therefore less important.

Then, you can include a third or fourth level of detail as you like. Images are highly beneficial since they provide a lot of information in a compact space. If you're not artistically inclined and need to print or cut out images if you need to.

At these levels, you can allow your brain to wander when it's needed, and then record all the information you'll need to remember later.

For some of the most important aspects, it may be helpful to put boxes around certain images and words in order to draw your attention to the important points. This will help you learn them.

It is possible to draw a colored line around a particular branch in your map of mind keeping the box close on the branch. The outlines will create patterns that your brain can perceive as clouds and assist you remember the ideas. You can apply the same colors on various branches to demonstrate that there is a link among the branch.

Mind maps are intended to be enjoyable to create So, enjoy the process and then get imaginative. The more you customize your mind map to create your own version more effective and useful it is for you.

Below, you will see an encapsulated mind map that is based on words:

If you sketch out the mindmap, you may make it bigger, adding images, colors, and much more to create an outline that not just appeals to you, but can actually work for you.

By using shapes, colors and symbols

The use of colors on your mind map can assist you remember the details you're mapping your mind with. What colors you select is entirely dependent on individual preference, however there are certain shades that can be used to refer to specific concepts:

Green is a sign of move. Consider traffic lights as an example. Green can be used to denote the action points.

Red usually means stop, therefore it could be used to refer to problems or issues.

Yellow is a color that can be used to indicate security or to identify things that require assessed.

Be aware that whichever colour scheme you decide to apply, you must to keep the same colors in your mind map; otherwise, it's going become very confusing quickly.

It is possible to use shapes to illustrate the ideas you have in your mental map. The suggested shapes differ between experts and experts, as well as between various software applications. Whatever you decide to use, no matter what software you are planning to use you must ensure that you are using the same shapes when you draw your mind mappings.

The primary idea that is at the top of your page is usually illustrated using the use of a circle or an oval. If you're using an image you could draw a circle, or an oval around the image.

You can make use of a star shape to represent actions or ideas to consider. Rectangular shapes are an excellent shape to wrap on top of your third and second levels of concepts. A triangle could be used to indicate a problem or concern (remember that many road safety signage are triangles).

If you're using software, you'll notice that every piece of software comes with its own suggested shapes that can be different.

When creating mind maps most people employ standard flow chart symbols since it's something students learn in school or have a good understanding of. If you're looking to make use of these, then they might be a good choice for you.

Whatever shapes, colors and symbols you decide to will use for your map of mind, be aware that you must be consistent throughout all of your maps. If you aren't constant, you could notice the mind map get difficult to comprehend and they lose their ability to aid in remembering things.

Color and shapes can be a effective way to increase the effectiveness of your mind maps. Make use of them effectively, and you will see your mind maps are more easy to remember and more efficient as you.

Learning and Note-Taking in Mind Maps

Mind maps are a great tool to assist you with study and note-taking of meetings, seminars or even books. Because they stimulate your brain and stimulate your creativity They aid you in learning to keep track of and organize facts and information. You are able to remember huge amounts of information by simply the visual representation of your mental map.

If you are creating a mind map to study and note-taking, you will require several minds maps (or layers within the software program) to cover the subject. one mind map could require a large sheet of paper.

If you begin with a single piece of paper, and you have the primary subject in the middle, and create your mind map for the higher level subjects and notes, you can create mind maps on different pieces of paper , each for a area within the topic. If you're using software to draw your mind map, you can add layers to your mind maps with one of the programs available or, if you prefer, simply connecting pieces of paper will work.

Others prefer to purchase a huge piece of paper and make one large mind map. The choice of whether to use this method instead of separate sheets of paper is completely dependent on what you are most at ease with.

If you're using a mind map to make notes, then you might decide to create a mental maps for every chapter in the book, for instance and then create a more comprehensive mind map that covers all the concepts and data inside the book.

Mind mapping for note-taking and studying is carried out similarly to an ordinary mind map, but you might wish to add a bit more information about it. It isn't necessary to write out a lot of information in your mind map, but you want enough information to help you remember the information , but be careful not to fill it with enough that you feel overwhelmed.

So , if you were using mind mapping to record your thoughts on the Olympics you could come up with something similar to this:

It is evident that the principal subject is located in the middle and then you will see chapters with chapter headings as well as more details about each chapter.

The most important thing here is the fact that every one of these points encapsulates something in just the form of a few sentences. If you see "New Stadium constructed" above, it brings back memories about an Olympic facility that was constructed and there are many more details about this.

"Held at East London" triggers other details, such as the event was at Stratford within East London, and then it is followed by more details.

Many people prefer writing notes in hand and later draw an outline of their mind using the notes. They can later refer back to their notes and also using the map to help them think.

Mind maps are an effective aid for studying. You will discover that it assists you to organize information in a concise manner. When you look at the mindmap, you are able to quickly recall large quantities of information due to the fact that your mind maps trigger release of information into your brain.

The use of pictures over words can be very effective when using a brain map to aid you in your study. Many people who use mind maps while studying say that they have a better ability to remember and organize information. They also report that they feel less stressed when it comes to studying. "Mind mappers" have found that their exams are less stressful because they quickly recall information and can connect the information to one another, which allows them to be able to answer questions with ease.

Chapter 9: Goal setting and Making Plans with Mind Maps

When you need to plan and setting goals Mind maps can aid you in the same way. They're a powerful tool that can help you keep all your thoughts laid out on paper to clearly visualize everything you must cover and complete.

The basic idea behind the creation of mind maps is similar to creating any other map of the mind, however, with the focus being on making goals and making plans.

Goal Setting with Mind Maps

Mind mapping to set goals can be accomplished using two methods.

1)One page - you make an entire page that you can put all of your goals on

2.) More Pages: You design one page for each area of your life that you are setting goals for.

The first step is to write your primary goal or even writing the word "My Goals" in the middle of the page before you begin to branch out by providing details about your goals. They can be broken down into several categories, such as:

It is possible to reduce these categories further by sub-goals and actions points for how you will achieve these goals:

It is possible to break these goals as many times as you'd like and help you develop the steps you can adhere to and reach your desired goal.

When it comes to goal setting using mind maps, images and images are very effective in fact. They can stimulate emotions in your brain and help to inspire you to reach your goals.

Consider what is the thing that would drive you most to purchase a brand new car? Would it be the phrases "a brand new vehicle" or a photo of the car you have in your desires?

The image will be more inspiring because it's emotionally charged and will ignite your passions in ways that words can't or won't.

Mind Maps To Plan Projects

It is also possible to make use of mind maps to help to plan projects. They can be used to organize projects for your work as well as for your job. You can also use them design projects for your home to do activities or home improvements. The usual guidelines of mind maps are applicable and can help clarify the scope of the project, and make sure you're focused on the tasks that are essential to complete.

The title of your project at the top of your page. After that, you write down the various aspects of your project around it, like Resources, Risks Timetable Aims,

Scope and any other information you believe you'll require.

After that, you can then write any other major points you believe you'll need to discuss. On the fourth stage, you will be able to go into specifics about each of the points.

After you've done your brain map,, you will have a visual representation of the entire project, which will allow you to see immediately everything that is connected to the project. It lets you connect the dots' among different components of the work, and identify opportunities or risks that you might not have noticed.

Below is the example below of a basic project plan in the form of a mindmap.

You can get into the level of detail you require with your mind map. You can also, for larger projects, you can create Mind maps to sub-projects or teams for projects which the team members can follow.

Mind maps are a great method to plan your project. It also provides clarity of thinking that would be otherwise only achieved through an extensive and lengthy document. They enable anyone to immediately get a better understanding of a project's scope and keeps the team on track to meeting the goals of the project and deadlines.

Outlining Writing Projects with Mind Maps
As you've probably guessed that mind maps are an excellent tool to unleash your creativity and organizing your thoughts and ideas. If you're an author or you're working on a project that you need for writing (whether for pleasure or business) Mind maps can be a great way to organize your thoughts and make sure you don't forget to include any details.

Although mind maps are an efficient way to organize your thoughts, only a few authors make use of them for their writing and outline. For writers, you can draw the mind maps on paper on a computer, or even whiteboards if you prefer. Writing books can be fluid, which means you might require changes to the mindmap you have created.

The mind map to do more than just writing out your book. It is also possible to use mind maps to design your marketing strategy in your publication, look up books that are similar to yours and many more.

Mind-mapping while outlining books works the same manner as if you were creating a standard mind map. The process is exactly the same beginning with the title for the book in the middle and then you draw an outline of your mind detailing the story, including the main characters and locations and also detailing chapters.

Here is a basic illustration below:

A mind map such as this will allow you to quickly and clearly visualize how you want to structure your novel and make sure that everything is in sync and flows properly. Since you can view the entire book outline in one location, you can quickly identify mistakes in your story or outline which need to be corrected.

If you have to write an outline of your book before you begin writing your book, an outline of your mind can be an excellent supplement to your proposal since the editor or the publishing house can quickly see what the book's content is in a single document instead of having to read through a lengthy book proposal. It is often an important difference when getting your proposal noticed as it's different and makes an impact. If you design your map attractive and include photos and colours, it looks stunning in the top in any proposal for a book.

If you're writing for business purposes, then the same rules apply.

Instead of writing out an outline, you describe the information that needs to be added the sections, the sources you require and the research that needs to be completed. The process is the same in the above outline, but you're focused on the report that you will need to write for your business.

Mind-mapping is an excellent tool for anyone with an assignment to write that must be completed. It doesn't matter if it's for leisure or business it is easy to see your entire work before you, and ensure that it's exactly what you need.

Problem solving, Brainstorming and Organising

We've discussed before the benefits of mind maps to stimulate your brain's entire system and let your mind be creative We're going to get into greater specifics on this.

If you are looking to solve any issue or organizing things Mind maps are a great tool to utilize because they allow you to manage any information very efficiently and then look at the whole mind map at once. It lets you focus on the entire issue simultaneously to allow you to easily connect the dots between various elements and develop innovative solutions.

The ability to tackle problems in a creative way is the reason why mind maps are now so widely used in all the different faculties of management. It is one of the tools that prominent business leaders regularly employ and also encourage their employees to utilize too.

The basic idea behind mind-mapping is the same regardless of whether you use it to think about to solve a problem, or plan something. The distinction lies in the way you organize your mind map.

Brainstorming with Mind Maps

Brainstorming is the method of thinking of ideas related to the subject. Most often, this is done with flip charts or a whiteboard and ideas are recorded mostly at random when they arise. It's not organized very well, and it can result in multiple ideas, and brainstorming could stall if all of the information is organised.

A mind map is exceptionally well for brainstorming. Write the subject you're mulling over on the paper (or on whiteboard or flip chart) and while you think about it and come up with ideas, you write them around the topic.

The ideas that come out could be third level concepts that are connected to ideas that are part of the subject you are contemplating. Other ideas could be based on these concepts at a third level.

The mind map allows ideas to be quickly organized with similar ideas . Using different colored lines and pens you can effortlessly connect diverse ideas.

For instance, you may be tempted to list items that are considered dangerous in red, things which are safe in blue and the ones which require further thought in orange or yellow.

Alternately, you can choose to utilize colors to indicate the urgency or importance of an issue, with red is the most important, while yellow is the next urgent, and green is not really urgent in any way.

This degree of organization right out of the gate allows brainstorming to become very efficient because there's no need to write down the ideas later. Once you've completed your brainstorming, you will have a complete mind map that you can immediately utilize. You can print it out and distribute it to each participant in the brainstorming session and depart with the identical idea of what transpired and what the outcome was.

When you are brainstorming mind maps can be used to aid in the whole process extremely well they are an instrument can be extremely beneficial.

Problem Solving with Mind Maps

In the process of solving issues, a mindmap is an excellent tool since it lets you approach any issue with creativity and combine various concepts to find a solutions that are creative to the issue.

If you're facing a challenge in your private life or in your professional life it is an effective tool you can utilize to get you to a solution you love.

The rules of mind-mapping are applicable here. You begin with a landscape piece of paper and pen. Then, in the middle, you'll record the issue, summarized in a few words.

While doing this, keep in mind that you're not trying to communicate your anger or to vent your frustrations over the issue. You're trying to find an answer to the problem and a mindmap can aid in keeping your mind away from the issue so that you can concentrate on the most effective solution.

In this way, you can define the issue and making sure that you're facing only a one problem, not multiple problems that are piled over each other. This will ensure that the issue is no longer overwhelming and begins to appear like it could be addressed. If you have multiple issues that require a mindmap for each of them could be a helpful tool to keep.

On the other side of the issue, you should draw out a different point, something similar to "Causes" In this case, you will then be able to write down the root of the issue.

You can then write a second known as "Resources" in which you describe the resources are needed to solve the issue. Perhaps you'll need to master the new skills, employ someone or hire someone. so that you can be able to solve the issue completely.

In the next step, you can write a section known as "Solutions" where you'll list the possible solutions to the issue you're dealing with.

Create a second document that explains what the problem will offer you after it has been solved. This will help you identify a solution to the issue, and may offer some incentive to find the solution.

Important issues you must consider when problem solving include:

* What's the Problem? Determine exactly what is the problem. If the problem is low sales, what do you know if it is an issue? Does everything sell poorly or is it only a specific item or two items?

* What's The Issue Not? It is important to define what isn't the issue - this will help to avoid confusion as well as pinpoint the root of the issue really is.

* I'm Having The Problem because - Why is there an issue? What is the of the problem?

* The Issue isn't Solved Since - This isn't a area to be worried about making excuses, but it's a place where you can begin to see the solutions tested but failed to work and

discover the root of the issue that exists in the beginning.

If you're solving problems for an organization, then you can examine the way other parts of the organization view the problem to gain a better understanding of the problem at hand.

This gives you an entire picture of the issue and then come up with a viable and practical solution to the problem that you currently face.

Mind Maps For Organization

Mind maps are extremely useful to organize because at the heart of mind maps is the concept of organization. They're a great method of visualizing information and arrange it in a manner that it aids recall help with problem solving, and help you connect dots between seeming disparate information.

If you're the kind of person with an office cluttered with Post-it notes and other papers with lists of things to do scattered all over the place, you could benefit by using mind maps to aid in organizing your life.

To organize the information for any topic, you just make a mind map of the subject. The standard procedure is to put the principal issue at the center and other subjects around it with decreasing importance. The use of colors, symbols, and images can prove to be extremely helpful since a picture can be worth more than a thousand words. Colors can aid in identifying items and help keep your focus on the important things that are at hand.

You can make one mind map to keep everything in order or create several mind maps that are specific to each space which requires organization.

Mind maps can be useful to not only organize your daily life but also to organize the information related to a particular topic. This is extremely useful when trying to cut down on the number of notes you keep on paper in order to quickly and quickly have a quick overview of the data you want to arrange.

Being able to view all of the information in one mind map can help you stay in the present and what you are most focused on. It is possible to are aware of the things you've done and what you're supposed to do and, often, you will find innovative solutions to your problems because of the organization you can get on the mindmap you have created.

If you are looking to arrange your work desk or your home life or the information needed to a project you're working on, mind maps are a an excellent tool to aid you in organizing your life.

Chapter 10: Tips to Utilize A Mind Map

When you're trying to solve a dilemma one of the most difficult obstacles is to break away from standard and conventional thinking. It is important to utilize your imagination and creative thinking to find the answer. Mind mapping can help you achieve this.

When you design your mind map of an issue, you put the issue in the middle and then come up with ideas around the problem. Begin by titling the branches from the center, using uncommon options that aid you in thinking in a new direction. You can try "Textures", "Animals", "Shapes", "People", "Transportation" and the list goes on. If you want to go further from these directions you may think of this:

Animals - How can beavers come up with a solution? It is obvious that a beaver isn't going to don a suit and tie , enter your office and solve your software issue

however, a beaver is an engineer? So, you could start thinking along the possibilities.
Textures What if we could make this from Burberry carpeting? Or slimly yummy grape jelly? You're not going to build an office chair using grape jelly - not even in the case of Lady Gaga, but the concept is to stimulate your thinking about things in "way off the beaten path" terms.

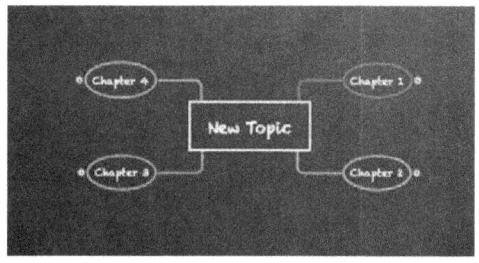

A lot of people who encounter mind mapping are unsure whether it's suitable appropriate for them. They might say that they are not artistically gifted or that mind mapping appears complicated and difficult to master. There are likely many reasons why someone might not want to take part in mind mapping. However, there are just as numerous, if not more benefits to studying and making use of mind mapping at school, at work and at home.

Mind maps are so called because it lets you "map" your ideas and thoughts making use of triggers, connections, as well as associations to inspire and spark thoughts. Mind maps take the thoughts from your brain to form something that is organized and clear.

Studies into the functions of the brain has proven that the brain functions best when it is with a connection-based foundation and connects every bit of data, memory, and concept to thousands and hundreds of concepts. When you create your mind map, it's very like the liner rather than circular capabilities of your brain. As a result, will allow you to master, memorize, arrange and solve problems much quicker and with less effort than using the simple tool for creating lists.

Problem Solving: Creating the mind map lets you think with an abundance of clarity on the problem you're trying to resolve. It assists you in identifying the connections between ideas and elements of an argument in order to come up with several solutions. Since you're not a part of the notion of a "ridged structure" using linear thinking, you'll discover it easier to integrate and organize any new information in a way that is feasible. Mind mapping offers a fresh perspective on the issue so that it is possible to identify the important questions and consider options within the bigger picture.

Creativity Mind maps are a fantastic tool to stimulate creativity, allow you to come up with fresh ideas through brainstorming. Additionally, the design of the mind map can assist you in getting a better understanding of the "big picture" and establish connections with greater clarity. This allows the creation of unlimited connections, ideas, and ideas for each subject created by the mind map process.

Planning and organizing Mind mapping is an immensely beneficial tool to have before starting an undertaking. Mind mapping can aid you in organizing the thoughts and ideas, and the data in "compartmentalized" and visually sized pieces that can ensure that you don't get stuck at some point in the course of completing the project.

Mind mapping has been proven to dramatically increase the recall of all kinds of data and information in comparison to traditional note-taking or list making. Mind mapping's unique blend of spatial-visual layout, colors and color allows working in a manner that the brain likes, which lets memory come naturally.

Learning - When utilized in the classroom the use of mind mapping has proven to generate renewed enthusiasm and excitement from students. Mind mapping can help instill the feeling of mastery over an ability that is new when utilized for different tasks.

Teaching - Mind mapping is a versatile tool that can be used for teaching, it is a great tool for applications in various kinds of academic contexts. Because of the visual cues of mind mapping, employing them in the classroom can be an effective method to improve understanding among students.

Collaborations Mind maps can be used for working with other people to create or enhance strategies, execute projects, and exchange information at a larger scale. Mind mapping allows for the connection of input from each participant in a unique and dynamic method.

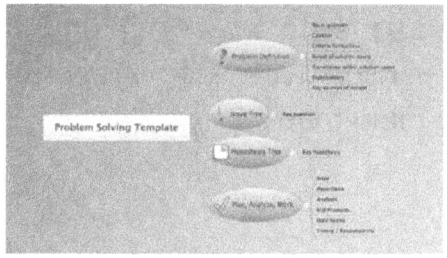

Mind Map Creating Techniques

Pen and Paper

The majority, if not all, people who are involved in mind mapping likely did it by using paper and pen. There are some extremely sophisticated mind mapping software that are available on your PC or laptop, and maybe even your smartphone. But, there are people who feel that it's impossible to beat the physical and mental connection of paper and pen when trying to resolve a problem or boost their creativity.

Benefits from Pen and Paper Mind Mapping

There are a myriad of advantages of drawing your own mind maps, just as there are benefits to using software programs for computers. This list is a summary of the advantages of using a pencil and paper to create mind maps, not any comparison with software programs to create mind maps.

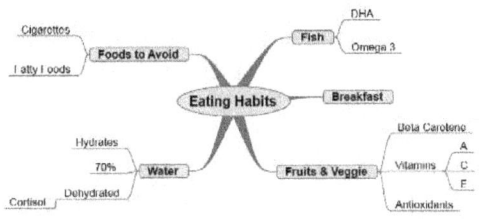

Pen and paper to make mind maps is a good way to ensure the possibility of being made whenever and wherever are. Because thoughts and "things to accomplish" are available in all times and are not always at the most suitable times, you are capable of capturing them quickly.

Pencils, pens and papers can be used almost anywhere, and mind maps can be drawn on almost anything and does not need to be on paper. Try creating mind maps on rolls of paper, canvas Flipcharts, wipe-boards, flipcharts, blackboards. Or even on blank walls The only limit is your imagination.

If you get started creating mind maps using pencil and paper you'll realize that they are extremely addictive. Mind maps can reveal your brain's power, experience and knowledge to help you discover new knowledge. Because you're using paper and pen which is a physical act it becomes memorable significant, memorable and meaningful aiding you discover and develop your imagination and also help you improve your thinking. Since the pictures and text are written in your personal handwriting, they help you remember your thoughts.

Style - Developing your individual style takes a bit of time and effort however, it is also enjoyable in the process of forming the first mind maps. The drawing ability and style is going to be as unique as the person who created the mind map. No two maps will be identical. The flexibility and versatility can be yours to make an mind map that twists and turns, looks dazzling and flashy, or easy and elegant or soft or sophisticated.

Unique - As you draw many mind maps over time, your own style will emerge. Like an artist with their distinctive signature and identifiable mark the mind maps you draw will be distinct in color appearance, style, and design. Don't get too excited over what you believe might be mistakes because they will become part of the scenery and could even be part of the process or solution that you're mapping out.

Direct - The physical process of creating a mindmap is immediate and progressing; instantaneously, you'll have direct flow from your mind to your paper, where you write down your thoughts and ideas before you forget them. Hand-drawn art stimulates your thoughts and emotions, as well as feelings, through your body and every sense to spark your imagination, and also your thinking to bring your uniqueness before you on paper.

Mind mapping using hand-drawing is fun, and it combines physical mental, emotional as well as the tactile, intimate and personal aspects. Its versatility taps into all parts of your brainpower and your senses. It will then work together to trace the route the map has drawn.

Computer

Like all things from at the start of history mind mapping has evolved in its evolution, growth and development. Technology has led to advancements in software that allow mind mapping to be done on your computer desktop tablet, laptop and mobile. Similar to those who prefer to create your mind map with pen and paper, there is many who prefer using the right software to create their mind mapping projects.

Benefits of Mind Mapping Software

There are numerous benefits to making use of mind mapping software. Teachers, business professionals students, students and anyone looking to become more efficient, productive or tackle a problem in their own lives could accomplish this by making use of a program specifically designed to help you map your mind.

Embedding - A variety of mind mapping software applications allow users to embed documents, links as well as notes and data within the map's structure in order to make it what can be described as the commanding visual file. This can be an assignment or task map that includes shortcuts and as you need to be able to backup your work when required. Most of the time the matter is whether your mind map is classified by Excel spreadsheet, an individual emails, Word document or web pages. All the details and information related to this specific assignment or project is linked to the mind map itself and is just a click away.

Storage Mind mapping software permits for the collapsibility and expansion of topic trees that can be added to the storage capacity for information. This allows larger tasks to be divided into a more manageable and controlled design.

Collaboration Mind mapping software programs that are designed to serve collaboration purposes. Mind maps created can be shared with office workstations and emailed to clients vendors, or anyone else who needs to see the final map, or team members that can be working on the map more or make annotations. Some software for mind mapping allows for multiple individuals working on the map in the same time.

Multi-functional - By nature, the mind mapping programs for computers are incredibly versatile and adaptable because they allow you to modify, delete, and re-arrange topics, lines, routes colors graphics, images or just about anything quickly and easily. Certain mind mapping software can let you track or save any modifications you make in the event that you decide to change your mind and need to return to the initial context.

Sharing One of the main advantages of mind mapping software is that it permits you to communicate with an audience, for example, in a conference or presentation format and in much better and more sophisticated ways than PowerPoint. If you've got questions and answers following the present of your mind mapping at end, you can incorporate your clients' questions, responses or suggestions right into your mind map and update it as needed and thereby increasing the interest of your audience in your concept.

Mind mapping with software programs for computers can provide advantageous on many levels for small and large enterprises with a significant number of employees, or just one employee. If integration with other software applications or technologies is necessary and you are looking for a mind mapping program, then this software could be the best kind of mind map tool to use.

Again, I need to ask a request .... If you've enjoyed this book. Would you please leave a review of this book? Thanks! I would love to add value to my next books!

How can you increase memory capacity?

If you're not gifted with the ability to capture images or any type of instant recall some people appear to have Mind mapping can increase your memory to levels of people you be jealous of.

The most important ingredient in memory is linking. It is the process of linking an object to be remembered to another idea or object that is called association. When your memory is able to provide an explanation for the thing you are trying to recall It puts an item's label so that it is easier to find or locate it. The same method can be used by linking to some different idea, and provide an appropriate label too. Another analogy is to think of your memory as a huge collection of books, each one with an image of the spine. It is bound to be much simpler for you to browse through the library and locate memories when they have the label.

Utilizing a mix of imagination along with animation and association you'll be amazed by how much better your memory will get in a very short amount of time. The most effective method to stimulate imagination and connection is to use mind mapping. It's an efficient way of thinking which precisely maps your brain.

They have the natural radiant structure which starts in the middle and utilizes arched lines images, colors, symbols as well as words and images as well as a set guidelines. While you are able to make your mind map the way you want This brain-friendly tool can assist you in increasing your ability to recall information quickly. Mind maps are straightforward and don't only impact your memory but aid in improving your ability to focus and develop your imagination. A vast amount of boring and boring information can be turned into an organized map that your brain naturally wants to follow. When you create an mind map that is colorful pictures, imaginative text, and the flow of space that will stimulate synergistic thinking, as well.

If you are beginning to improve your creativity You are developing the capacity to generate unique and original ideas, concepts, and ideas and, in turn, you're increasing your capacity to recall more and more. Since creativity and memory are both mental processes that are perpendicularly similar and perform best when you are engaged in imagination and association.

Mind Mapping to Enhance Memory

If you take a look at the mind map, you'll be able to see that they use just one word or two per line. which is a keyword, and not a great deal of text. This is due to the fact that you need an important, brief word that can trigger your memory when you are creating or going over your map of mind, not tons of words.

Mind maps are created to help encourage connections and connections. The creation of these connections as well as associations between concepts and other things is a crucial element to increasing memory. When you make your own mind map you're not just enhancing the connections between objects, but you're also laying out these connections clearly and as a visual reference on the page that is your face. With the help of images and colors mind maps stimulate your mind and are the key to a better memory.

A Great Tip

The majority of people are aware that in order in order to commit something to memory, you have to review it at minimum three times. Mind maps allow you to easily review information over and over again. The mind also functions by connecting things and mind maps work in the same way. Mind maps help to create connections between objects.

If you're using mind maps for studying such as a course it is possible to follow your teacher's instructions, take notes that are linear, then transfer them onto the mind maps. You have read the material three times. But, you could move things up a notch by revisiting your mind map for two or three times prior to the exam or even bring the map into your group study and build on the information with them. In addition, the fact the information is presented in the most basic form is helpful to you retain the knowledge even more. It is also important to note that any mindmap is designed to illustrate the connection between different things will assist you to absorb and comprehend the information well.

Revisit the mindmap on a regular basis and you'll see that the information contained in the mind map will be absorbed by your brain. It will also provide an entirely new perspective on the information contained within your mental map. It can also assist you to reevaluate things as they evolve and help you remember things you might have lost track of.

Mind Mapping Example

To make notes using mind maps, you mark the topic you're studying or wish to remember as the main idea and then , starting from the center you create a branch by adding supporting information. This is accomplished by drawing lines from the center, and then marking them with details or details about the central idea. Then you draw secondary branches to support the main branches. Then you expand further and more detailed notes of information when you come across it or find it.

Here's an example:

This mind map summarises the part concerning eating habits and how they assist in improving memory. Since the focus is on food habits and eating, it is best to place it in the middle.

In each of the primary branches we also included additional information in secondary branches. For instance under the category "fruits and vegetables," we listed the information said regarding their benefits, namely that they are a great supply of beta carotene and vitamins A, C, and E as well as antioxidants. In"water," the "water" branch we highlighted the crucial information about drinking water.

Then, you start by establishing the basic idea at the center Then you extend outward , adding supporting and subordinate specifics. There are no limitations in the amount of support or subsidiary branches you can create.

Making use of mind notes with maps provides many benefits. One advantage is that these kinds notes tend to be more visually appealing and the information that is presented in a visual format is simpler to recall. Additionally, notes made in this manner can help you organize information, making it easier to for you to comprehend. It also helps in retaining information.

Mind maps are a great tool for planning your day. You are able to do more than just take notes. Mind maps are great to study, brainstorming planning, writing, and brainstorming.

Chapter 11: Ask for Assistance with Your Ideas

We are not perfect, and our capabilities are limited by what our bodies are able to accomplish and our understanding of the things we wish to accomplish. In this regard, it is essential to seek assistance to improve our thinking and ideas in order to more efficiently organize them. The man is a social being and that is the reason we must seek out assistance from others to improve the best. Also, there is the possibility of making use of technology. The internet, while not 100 100% reliable, is an extremely effective source of information can be used.

Tip 1: Contact your friends

It's really simple. I'm certain that your acquaintances will be eager to assist you, so why not try asking them when you feel like you're stuck or don't know what to do. It won't do anyone any harm and it won't be an issue to get them to respond therefore you've got nothing to lose. If they don't know the answer, you can simply find the answer using various means. It is at least a good idea to try the most straightforward method first.

Tip 2: Make Use of the latest technology

As I mentioned technology plays a significant role in sharing information in the present. The majority of information is now electronic from bibles to dictionaries to almanacs to more it's just a matter of choose the right one. You can get a lot of information simply by searching it. However, you must be aware of details that might be fake such as Wikipedia pages. Wikipedia pages. Because they can be altered by anyone who has access, there is a chance that some are incorrect. You could also cross-reference your information you have already gathered about your ideas to other websites to ensure that they're correct.

Tip 3. Read

If you're not knowledgeable about the technical aspects of life , you could go back to the old-fashioned way of thinking and read books which will help expand your understanding about your ideas and thoughts. Libraries are still in the world and libraries are full of books that will aid you in gaining an idea of what you'd like to achieve or how you would like to turn your ideas and thoughts reality. In addition, reading provides an added benefit of expanding your vocabulary and helping keep your memory sharp.

Tip 4: Talk to professionals

It's similar to asking acquaintances, but you can be certain that the people you ask are aware of the subject matter they're discussing. While this chapter in this book (Step 5: Get Assistance with Your Ideas) may not seem to be related to the theme of the book, I'm able to be sure that it not. It is essential to learn more about your thoughts and ideas so that you can, eventually, put them into action without difficulty.

Chapter 12: What to Customize A Mind Map

Although I've only covered only the essentials in the final chapter, I'm hoping you do not get the impression that there's not much to the process that is Mind Mapping. There is no such thing. There are hundreds of thousands of ways to draw the similar Mind Map with the same entries, and every version has a different impact on your brain. This is the reason Mind Map can be used to fulfill two different purposes: creative thinking that is free in nature and is described as the "right brain" activity as well as an organized and analytical mind, that can be more focused, and is is a "left brain" activity. Now that you understand how to draw an Mind Map and hopefully using it in your everyday life we'll discuss how you can try out the different elements of a Mind Map.

Color

The Mind Map can be described as a visually-oriented method and color is a crucial component of your sense of sight. While a black-and-white Mind Map is much more efficient than conventional notes that are linear with colors, using color in the Mind Map opens up a completely new range of possibilities. It is possible to use various hues for different subtopics or use them to draw attention to certain areas. If there's an established connection between a particular keyword and a particular color (such as orange-carrot, elephant-gray or Democratic party blue) it could create connections in your brain stronger.

Size

The size of the text is another significant visual aspect. You can make the keywords which are closest to the topic in order to indicate the hierarchy or even emphasize a certain word by making it larger than the other words that are on the same level. Alongside the words it is possible to alter the width that the lines are drawn. Some people may find applying a uniform weight to the lines to be more effective however, some might prefer to start thicker, gradually reducing the thickness as it gets further towards the middle, much as the branches do in nature.

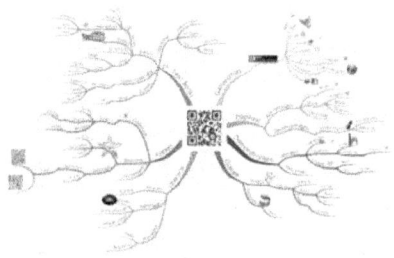

Figure 3-1. A sample of Mind Map with fairly uniform line weight and size for keywords.
Figure 3. A sample of Mind Map with varied keyword size and weight

Shapes

You may also employ different shapes such as circles ovals and rectangles to classify the concepts , or highlight some over other. Consider the way a flow chart is created: it makes use of diverse shapes to symbolize different kinds of actions (start and end actions, decision and start). Shapes are an excellent way to organize your thoughts, along with dimensions and color.

Shapes or lines?

Two ways to write keywords. One option is to write them in an elongated line, thus making the lines continue as they stem from the keyword at its center. Another alternative is to draw them in a particular shape or in the empty space with no lines. Here's an example that will show the two possibilities in one map:

Figure 3-3. Keywords are written on a form or on the line.

I would say this falls under an area of individual preferences. Although Tony Buzan claims that keywords should be written on lines but I prefer simple circles and a thin line to ensure that it doesn't block with the keywords visually or wrap any time surrounding the keywords. It is possible to make a hybrid of both. It is possible to write the keyword in a form, and add some annotations as needed over the connect line similar to the concept maps that I briefly discussed in Chapter 1. Whatever method you decide to use I would advise you to think creatively about the process and come up with innovative ways of organizing and representing your ideas.

Symbol

Here's where the fun starts. Only humans have the ability to interpret things as representations of something else, which is to employ symbols. The language and words that are that are used within Mind Maps are a type of symbol also. Because Mind Map triggers your brain to activate more intuition The use of symbols is not just an entertaining addition for the Mind Map but also can boost your creativity. Start with common symbols like questions marks or the the plus sign, and then begin making your own. If you implement Mind Map into your everyday daily life (which I highly suggest that you do) You will appreciate it if you can substitute some of the common concepts or ideas by using symbols.

Images

Another enjoyable way to alter your Mind Map, you can create or paste images to depict a thought. If you're working on drawing a hand-drawn Mind Map and you have good drawing abilities, this will be entertaining and stimulating to your brain. If you're not able to draw, don't be worried. There are programs for computers that provide you with lots of clip-art illustrations and you do not have to create it on your own. Chapter 5 will provide more in-depth information about computers-based Mind Mapping. No matter what method you choose to use this is an effective method to make your Mind Map more "alive" and more effective.

Different line shapes

Alongside the thickness I previously mentioned You can also play around with the different shapes of connecting lines. It is possible to make them more or less long, straight or curly or their space becoming wider or narrower, based on the importance of the concept in question or the goal of Your Mind Map. Also you may find yourself using straight lines and standard fonts when preparing a course material to take a test, whereas you may prefer to utilize curvy lines and funny fonts while thinking about your story.

Figure 3-4. A free-form example Mind Map

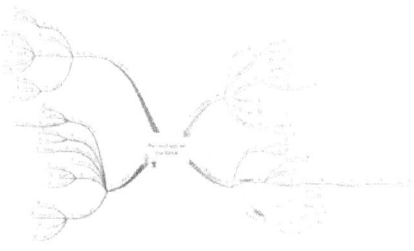

Figure 3. An example of "organized" Mind Map

The overall layout of the Mind Map

By combining all the elements (and even more, if have other ideas) of personalization discussed in this article It will be helpful for you to visualize what the general layout is of your Mind Map and how you can make it work for the purpose you're making it. If, as we mentioned previously, you're trying to organize notes from lectures and transform them into an Mind Map which explains the information clearly and succinctly, you may want to keep it neat and tidy with no oddities, or omissions. If you're creating a presentation and are trying to utilize Mind Maps to present your ideas, and you want them to be used as a Mind Map as a powerful and persuasive communication tool then you should employ some color and appropriate images and symbols. In this instance you'll have to play around with various arrangements of ideas to determine the most effective and most convincing method however, most instances, you'll use the basic chronological format for the notes of lecture.

The main goal here is to determine the best fit for your needs and the goals you are trying to accomplish. The first step is to figure out your own personal preferences and using them to increase the efficacy in Mind Maps. Mind Map for you. The second is about the goal of using the Mind Map and the specific use that you can make of your Mind Map for a specific moment. Your personal preferences are what you will need to test yourself. For this reason I'll go over them and go over some of the most effective uses for Mind Maps in the next chapter. Mind Map in the next chapter. While reading it will be easy to be amazed at how the possibilities for a Mind Map are almost limitless However, you will also begin to think about which style that Mind Mapping would be best for each situation. You can also see several instances of Mind Maps done in different styles in the appendix. It will be clear how the concepts that are discussed in this chapter play out in real-world examples.

Chapter 13: Digital Mind Maps

Software for mind mapping is a great option for those who want to utilize the idea regularly. Mind mapping software applications are distinct from online mind mapping software since they must be downloaded via the Internet and then saved as programs to the Mac computer or computer.

With the latest software and web-based applications The entire process can be accomplished quickly and carried with you.

A few of the mind mapping software applications listed below are free. Others permit users to download and use their software for no cost on a trial basis and some will be available at the cost of.

However, as everything else it is the case that what you pay for is generally what you get. The software that is free as described below are fantastic instruments for both professional and personal tasks and techniques for problem solving However, the paid versions typically have additional options and features that free versions don't have.

However, every one is worth a shot This is the reason we've reviewed some of the most effective applications available online and available to download, as well as some basic information on their installation and usage and the price associated with each along with its pros as well as cons and the operating system requirements.

In the final analysis it's up to you to choose which fits your personal or professional requirements.

6.1 Web-based Mind mapping tools

Mind mapping apps that are web-based are available on the internet without downloading software. There are numerous tools to choose from, some of them are free , while others are available for a trial period of 30 days and then a monthly subscription.

A lot of these choices offer apps for download to enable mapping while on the move much more convenient.

It is possible that you prefer using pen and paper in the end however, you'll never be able to tell until you try the digital realm too.

The picture below shows how the software for mind mapping is that is utilized on tablets as well.

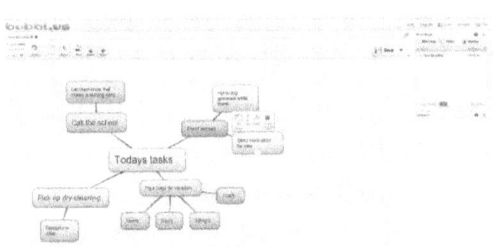

6.1.1 Bubbl.us

http://bubbl.us

(Most of the mindmaps used in this book were drawn using bubbl.us)

Bubbl.us is a completely free online tool for mind mapping that is simple to use without learning complicated procedures or steps. It lets users create Mind diagrams for brainstorming and mapping quickly. To access the site, you have be able to install an up-to latest flash viewer.

The website is easy and simple to use. You can make a mind map that doesn't require images, and it is possible to save the map as JPEG directly to your computer. There aren't many options to master and this makes the program suitable for daily use.

You can try the tool at no cost for a small amount of maps prior to being asked to upgrade.

If you're in search of an application that will give you to take a greater degree of control, then this might not be the program for you.

6.1.2 Mindomo

Visit Mindomo at http://www.mindomo.com

Mindomo is a website-based Mind mapping tool with many more features than bubbl.us however it's somewhat more complicated to use. A disadvantage is that it's free , with the creation of just 3 maps. After that, you'll have to will be charged between $6.00 to $29.00 each month.

However, one of the main benefits you'd like a web-based mind mapping tool will offer is collaborative map-building and the capability for two users to edit maps simultaneously but Mindomo does not yet provide this feature.

Users can pick from a range of styles for layouts, which allows for some personalization of the display.

Similar to Bubbl.us The program was specifically designed to use the most recent flash viewer. Mindomo users can modify the appearance and appearance of their Mind map by using various designs, fonts, styles as well as colors and so on.

6.1.3 MindMeister

Visit MindMeister at http://mindmeister.com/

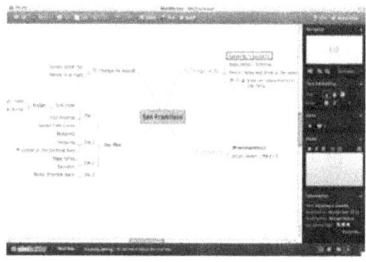

It doesn't have the fancy effects of Flash and the default display relies more on the data you've captured and not so much on forms, gradients, as well as animated effects.

MindMeister offers all the essential features you would expect in a web-based application similar to this. The keyboard navigation is, in general, easy and users can use the tab button for adding a kid to the program, the enter key to add siblings and the Arrow keys to move around the diagram in a smooth manner.

Saving is done automatically and there is no effort from the user. Nodes can be moved around with Drag and Drop. Users can share using the option of view or write access. It supports the ability to import data from FreeMind as well as Mindjet's MindManager and the export option to either an RTF outline or GIF image.

6.2 The Mind mapping Software

Mind mapping programs are available for purchase to install onto your PC. If you are using the mind mapping software on frequently then this could be your most suitable option. It's much more reliable and the license can be bought for several computers.

The maps you create by your business or home will share the same features and style; this is particularly important for companies that wish to create a consistent appearance. Maps created from a variety of web sources may appear messy to potential clients.

6.2.1 Imind map

www.imindmap.com

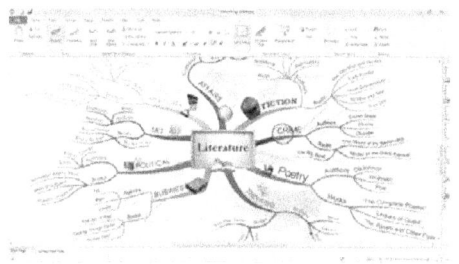

iMindMap is a piece of software that was created by the man who created the mind map himself Tony Buzan. The program is compatible with Mac computers as well as PC's.

Presently, iMindMap is the leading mind mapping software that is available online because of its flexibility and adaptability. iMindMap was created to be practical and innovative. More than 250 million people make use of iMindMap to think and work with greater effectiveness.

iMindMap users can make stunning maps in just minutes. It's the only application that lets you create 3D mini maps for greater visibility. The result is beautiful and gives your work a professional and polished edge.

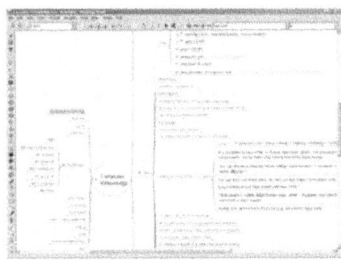

It can take time to master the program however, and users can anticipate spending a an adequate amount of time watching instructional videos and testing different features of the software.

After you've created some maps, you'll be able to get a feel for the program and it will be an integral part of your professional and personal growth.

6.2.2 FreeMind

http://freemind.sourceforge.net/wiki/index.php/Main_Page

FreeMind is an application for mind mapping developed specifically for Mac as well as Windows users. It is written in Java. It allows users to organize their thoughts onto the screen, and also to join them in order to create larger images.

Users can design their primary notion (which FreeMind refers to as the root node) and put it on the page and then create siblings or child notes that relate to it.

FreeMind has a variety of features, including various icon styles and color formats to allow you to create distinctive maps that visually well-organized.

FreeMind software can make use of hyperlinks. These allows you to connect documents and websites with your maps.

Maps can be exported in various formats such as HTML PDF as well as JPEG.

While FreeMind is fairly flexible and particularly helpful however, it doesn't allow users to drag and click their nodes. It is necessary to insert nodes manually, or with hot keys, which is a bit frustrating for those familiar with the ease of the latest software applications.

If FreeMind was to redesign their interface to include an intuitive drag-and-drop feature It would dramatically enhance its user-friendliness and versatility.

6.2.3 ConceptDraw

http://conceptdraw.com/mindmap

ConceptDraw is a remarkable software suite created by Ukrainian-based CS Odessa. It is compatible to Windows as well as Mac operating systems. ConceptDraw allows users to draw Mind maps, sketch ideas, and to organize thoughts and data.

It's a bit expensive, but it offers a variety of capabilities. ConceptDraw lets you track the deadlines, milestones and costs that are associated with a particular project.

Its layout makes it simple to mimic popular word processing software. The toolbar and functions appear to be like something you've used before.

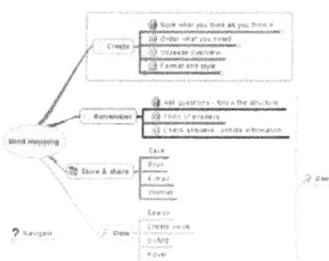

6.2.4 Freeplane

http://freeplane.sourceforge.net/wiki/index.php/Main_Page

Freeplane is an open source and flexible Mind mapping software program that is Windows compatible and totally available for use at no cost.

The program may need you to take some time learning to utilize the features it offers however, once you master it you'll be happy that you took the time!

It is loaded with features that are loaded. It can assist in creating Mind mapping an enjoyable and enjoyable experience which you can make use of for personal, educational professional, and personal use.

Chapter 14: The Benefits Of Making Use of Mind Maps

You should now be able to get a handle of how beneficial brain guides are. They can be modified in a way that you can use them to do almost anything. Additionally, mind maps can help you open your brain and be more clearly. There exists a theory that relates to how humans optimally think. It's called "Entire Brain Thinking'. Planning for psyche may cause a whole cerebrum thought to take place that allows people to think more clearly and faster.

In essence, what the "Entire Brain Thinking' hypothesis states is that people are able to think in four distinct ways:

Logical -- Concentrates upon the factual information and final result

Creative - Looks at the whole picture, and likes to be entertained

Practical -- Helps organize and follow-up

Relational -- Tune into their personal and the feelings of others

Certain individuals are more reliable, and some are more imaginative. Certain people are generally more effective, whereas others will depend on their moods. However that we can all think in any of these methods, although at times we'll generally be able to think in one direction over the other. These kinds of intuition operate in harmonious co-operation.

Intelligent thinking is connected with focusing on the central problem. This is the type of thinking that leads us to defend concepts such as in the case of a=b and b=c. the absolute necessity of the equivalent 'c' also. Ingenious reasoning allows us to understand the overall plan of things. This is also the part of us that allows us to be able to play and have an enjoyable time.

The social component of our reasoning allows us to be aware of our thoughts and feelings in the same way as of other people. This is also connected with how we handle the vast and insignificant aspects of our daily life. So, by following this line of thinking, we are able to identify with various thoughts and ideas in like the way we are able to identify with other people. In addition, logical reasoning lets us compose and then move.

The reason the psyche maps are so amazing is because they draw on the various kinds of thinking. Brain planning allows you to discern how different thoughts and ideas fit together in a way that is legitimate such as. Additionally, there is a visual aspect to mind maps that allow you to see the complete image' first. This makes use of the creative aspect of our thinking. Mind planning also allows us to create ideas and experiment with concepts. It also helps to develop our creativity in that way too.

Social reasoning is the reason we can see the links between different ideas and articles, which was just established as a vital part of that is brain-based planning. The ability to see these connections allows us to rethink our thoughts and form our ideas in a rational way. Social reasoning is also a factor when we're delineating the boundaries of things. The majority of the information we come up with is based on the way we feel about things as our psyche's creative inclination is sifting out ideas. It is our ability to think in a way that makes us want to arrange the data into a mental map in order to make it a usable structure and move.

As you can see, these kinds of reasoning operate and interact with one another and are connected to each other. Brain planning lets us access all these kinds of thinking and allow them to function more effectively and in a way that is more amiable to one another. These thought patterns can be tapped into when someone is looking at the information on the map of the psyche that is that brain maps are easy to learn from. They allow the whole mind to be locked into. In essence, it is able to take into consideration all brain thinking.

The whole of the different elements of what it takes to be human is communicated to by the brain map. Brain maps are designed in this manner. They are designed to be utilized in different ways with the intention that all kinds of objectives can be developed by using the use of them. Their design designed to incorporate various kinds of reasoning allows you to think on a much higher level that you normally would with otherwise.

If you've never used the psyche map before then you must take a look at it today. Simply take a few sheets of paper, and begin your own journey by experiencing the concept for yourself. In this way, you will are aware in fact what a guide to your brain can do for you prior to moving forward. There's a vast number of ways this kind of arrangement and interpreting data can help you improve your company, your relationships and also your personal life.

The benefits of using Mind Maps

All in all, specifically what are the main points that you should consider when using mind maps? The most important thing is that they are more effective with the mind than various tools. The method that psyche maps function is a viable option as we think as humans. We all require the equalization of their brains and associations, and brain maps provide the means to accomplish this. They can help us enjoy and creative sides as well. The way in that people deal with big issues is either to tackle the issues in small increments or to find a way to complete huge tasks. The psyche maps allow us to achieve all of this through empowering the way we think.

Brain maps also advance the capacities. This is because of the fact that you will turn out to be more enthralled by them than with other devices. This is because they are able to'spring up even though they're essentially notepads. They also help stabilize the cerebrum and remove any obstacles that hinder different parts of our brain to function in harmony against one another.

The various benefits of using mind maps across various instruments is that they clearly show connections increase creativity, improve efficiency, and make it easier and faster to make notes and review them. The reason is because mental planning can be a way to capture data in creative and visual ways. In other words, it could use different colors and shapes to communicate to different groups or levels. This allows information to be seen immediately, and even in the beginning. This is an enjoyable creative, imaginative, and visual type of learning. Anyone who teaches will inform you that your mind is at its most active when information is presented for entertainment in only creative, imaginative, and visual ways. This is the primary reason for psyche maps to be amazing learning tools.

The disadvantages of Mind Maps

There are some limitations to using mind maps as well. In some instances, mind maps can cause people to focus too much. This is why it is sometimes necessary to take a step back to gain an objective look at the data in order to make it more positive. In essence, you are at the moment you're working on an MRI, you're taking things apart at the point of being so small that you don't even discern the overall plan.

Another issue with minds maps is the fact that they often times reserve more effort to sketch out in the event that you're facing an unpredictable problem. This is due to the fact that using mind maps, you begin working with a limited area. The more complex issues generally require more than one mind map or a more extensive one that might not be worth your time and energy. Just think of the brain map that was created specifically for Boeing Aircraft. It was 25 feet long. In this case it was a good idea despite the difficulties and hassle.

In the end, some people have difficulty understanding how to use mind maps. There are people who do not think they will make enough use of it to warrant an investment in understanding the best way to utilize it. This is okay, but most people are able to do this with no issue. If people do it, they in typically discover that it helps them to do so in a massive way.

There are instances where people become overwhelmed by the software as well. Despite the fact that psyche-planning programs for automated use are beneficial however, they don't usually require these extra features to create an impressive brain map. This is evident in situations where you're just trying to arrange or break up problems for your own requirements. There's nothing wrong with writing down your thoughts on paper to be used to meet your needs or creating a mind diagram on a poster board in order to share your thoughts to each person.

The benefits outweigh the disadvantages.

In some instances, it does not justify the effort and time required to make use of mind maps, especially if there are other instruments which are better suited to your job or way of organizing. Mind maps are incredibly useful and offer many advantages over various instrumentation for conceptualizing and arranging, in spite of. The benefits of using mind maps are far superior to the limitations generally. They can help you think more clearly and allow you engage in more intelligent discussions with other people too. Additionally, the end outcome of a brain-planning meeting will generally be superior than other similar types of exercises.

The process of planning your thoughts in psyche not only causes the mind to imagine and think of revolutionary ideas rapidly however, it also expands your brain to ensure to function efficiently. While you're thinking, you're writing down your ideas. Additionally, once you're finished, you are able to return and revise or alter your data however you like. Finally, once all of this is completed you'll have a translatable collection of thoughts and realities you can present your arrangement, discuss ideas, or even share other people with.

Chapter 15: Examples of Mind Mapping and Mind Mapping Software

Explanations and examples of many different approaches that people might take.

After we've examined the steps to create mind maps Let's take some time to examine some other examples in detail. We'll first take a examine some other examples of mind maps. A majority of those who make mind maps for businesses educational institutions, non-profits, or even for business are using a the software for mind maps. We will mention the software in these instances and also provide the URLs of their websites as an appendix.

Some examples of Mind Mapping
Examples of Business:
http://www.matchware.com/en/templates/mind-map-revenue-forecast.php

The mind map in question is a forecast of revenue for a business from various locations across the globe. Obviously, this would be a large multi-national corporation and this mind map would be developed by the Accounting/Financials Department. Let's take a look at how they constructed the mind map.

The first thing you'll be able to see is that the mind map you see here is not so fluid as other mind maps we take a look at. It is very organized (as it is the result of a highly structured profession) yet it adheres to the guidelines in mind mapping.

1.In the center lies the main idea or the problem. This is the Revenue Forecast contrasts the budget against the actual amount and an estimate of +/- figure for the whole business. Also, there's a note and an attachment in the middle. This is one of the greatest attributes of mind mapping and that is the capability to add supporting documents and hyperlinks on the map.

2.In this mental map the biggest branches coming out of the center are regions of the globe that have offices of the company. The branches are named North America, South America, Asia and Europe. These are the principal areas that generate income for the company. Each of these locations displays the budget, actual as well as +/-. It is evident that there is a note on North America, but no documents are attached to each of the four branches, and only North America has a note.

3.Now each branch is broken in three pieces. These are sub-locations of the larger one and provide the budget, real as well as +/-. Also, notice that US has a note on it. There are no other branches with notes.

4.I am certain that there may be more smaller twigs coming off of all the twigs in #3 that could be sent to states/provinces or cities. If a new place is added onto the map, it's extremely easy to add that new information to the mind map, and be able to see everything in one glance.

Think about the typical annual revenue reports that we're used to seeing , regardless of our own businesses, or if we belong to a non-profit or social organisation or sit on any board. We're used to seeing the flow of data that would display the same information on the form of a spreadsheet which had been read left-to-right or an outline which had to have to be read starting from the top and ending at the bottom. The latter of these ways of organizing the data let you view in a glance the entire financial picture of your business during the month.

For instance, using this mind map, you will see that this business had income for the month that was 2.8 percent more than the budget. It's a great thing I'm certain, however it never provides the complete picture. What exactly did this new income come from? Did every single location exceed or meet their budgets? In a traditional spreadsheet you may have to look through three or four pages deep into the report to discover this data. By using this mind map, you can observe quickly the fact that North America and Europe over did while Asia as well as South America under performed. Additionally, you can observe that the majority of your production over came from Germany however the most under-production was found in Peru.

Consider how long it will be to pull this data from a typical financial report. Although we mentioned at the start that this mind map was somewhat well-organized and not as fluid and free flow as other mind maps might be, it's nevertheless remarkably sophisticated in showing all the information in an instant. It's easy to see the reason why providing traditional financial data in this manner is efficient and increases efficiency and productivity.

Let's move on to another type of scenario. Let's take a look at an example which is actually a mental map of the way to approach using mind maps. This one is more interesting to examine, more inventive and colourful, and takes users to the exact spot when it comes to organizing information in a manner that is simple to understand and to act upon.

http://mappio.com/

This mind map the same manner as we did in the prior one. This mind map is based on the concept or image of the The Team Mapping Method. This group will come up with a method to do mind mapping as a team or group.

1.Once again, in the middle of the page, there is the most significant idea/image, or in this case the goal. This mindmap in contrast to the previous instance, you can notice a lot of imagination as well as color and enjoyment in the placement of the main idea in the mind map.

2.The parts of the mindmap represent the steps to be completed in order to arrive at group mapping. The branches are:

* Defines the topic
Individual concept maps
* First consolidation
* Second consolidation
* Prioritization
* Take Action

One of the interesting aspects of the mindmap is the fact that the branches are identified by numbers 1-5, and the tasks that need to be completed follow this chronological order. However, this is not the case for all maps of mind. Actually, it's more likely that it is not.

www.ingramcontent.com/pod-product-compliance
Lightning Source LLC
Chambersburg PA
CBHW071838080526
44589CB00012B/1041